Emoji : Coloring book

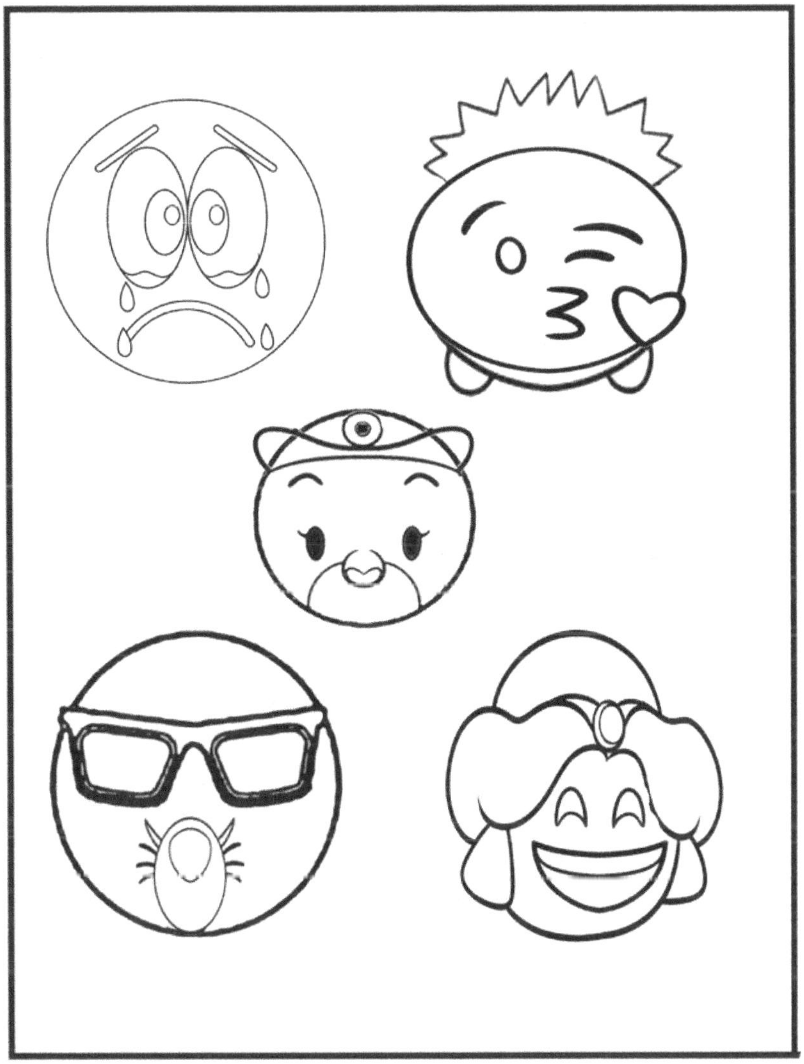

PJ King

Emoji Coloring Activity Book

Copyright: Published in the United States by PJ King
Published January 2018

ISBN-13: 978-1983554681

ISBN-10: 1983554685

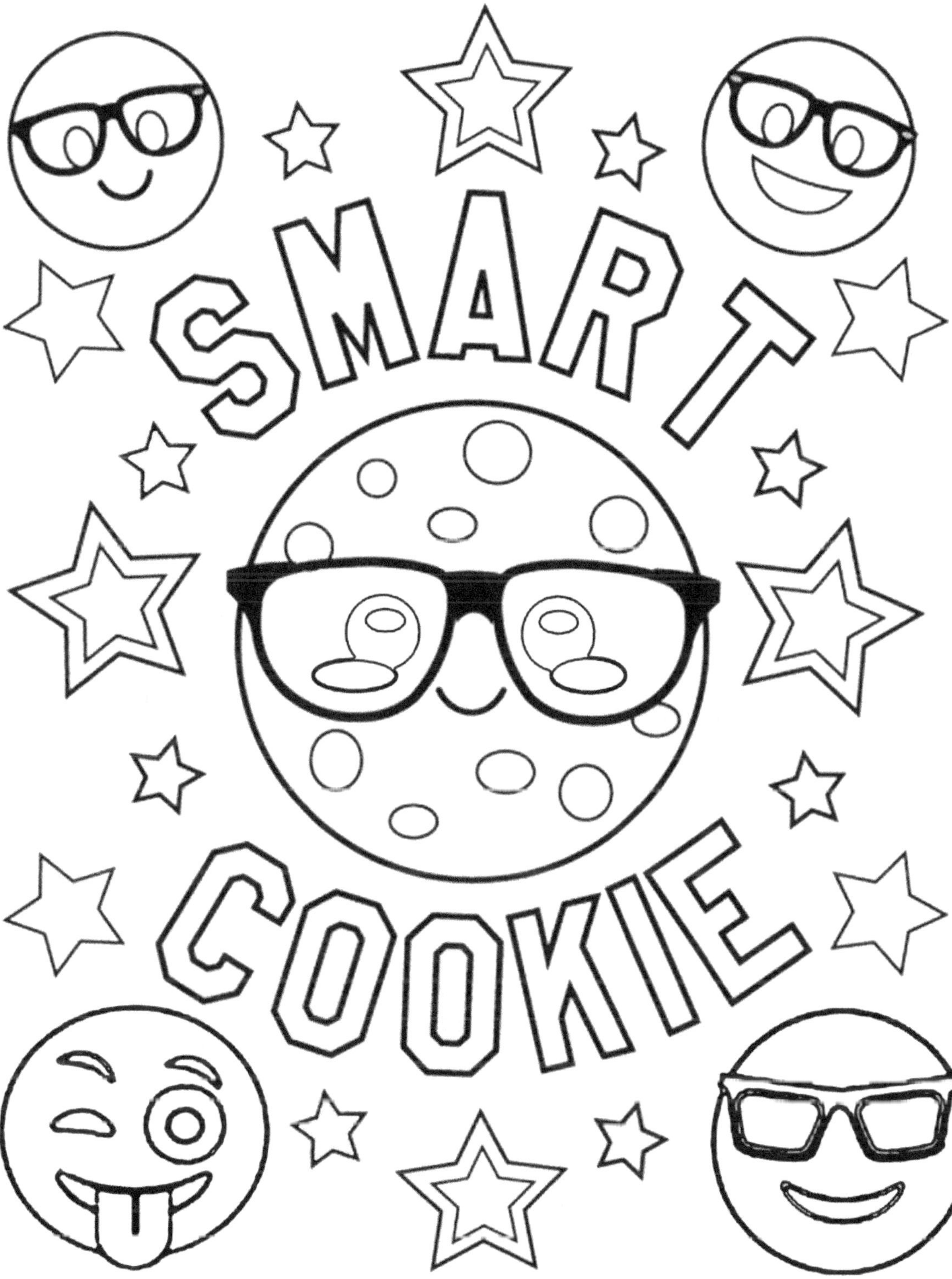
SMART
COOKIE

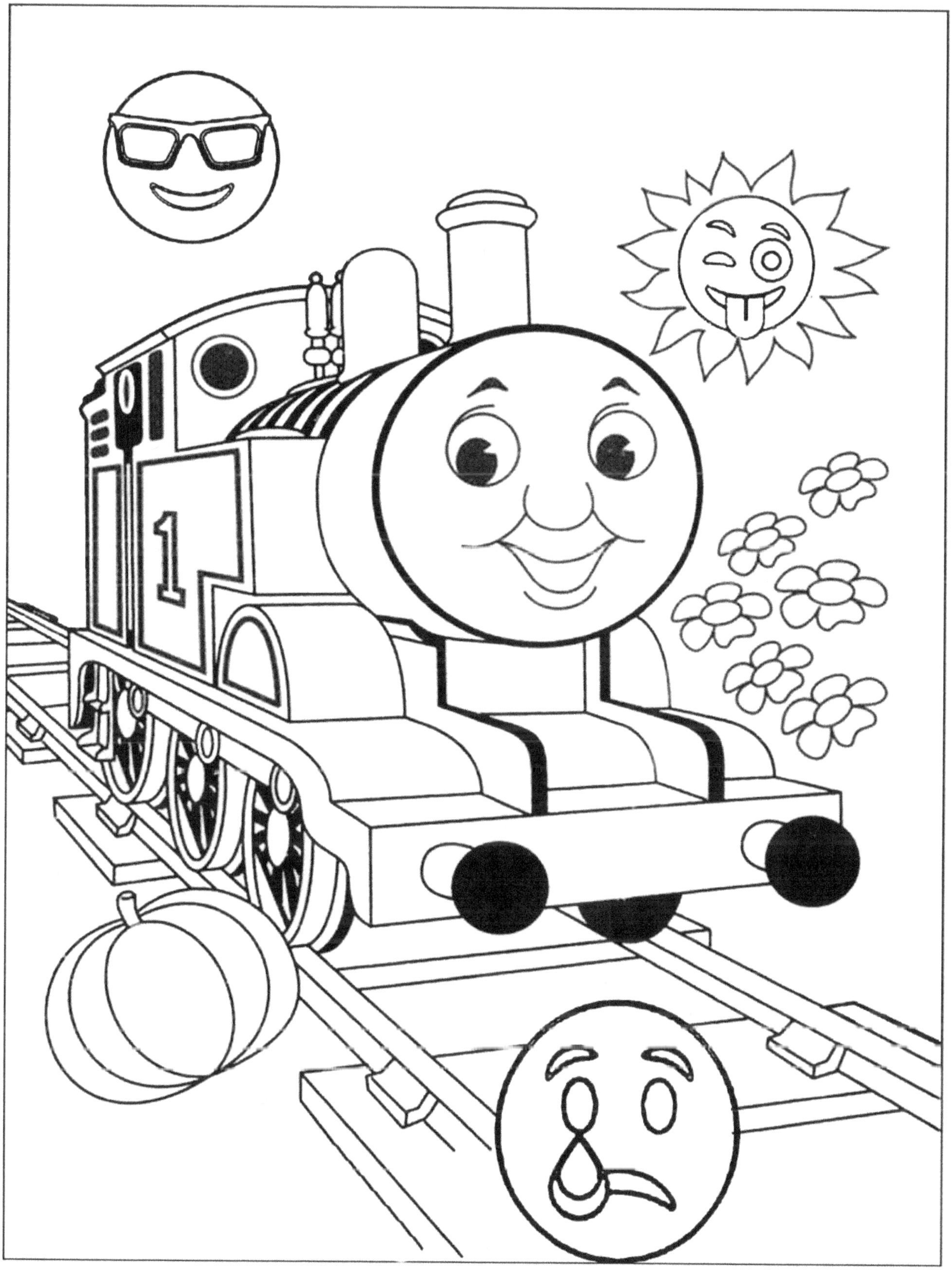
1

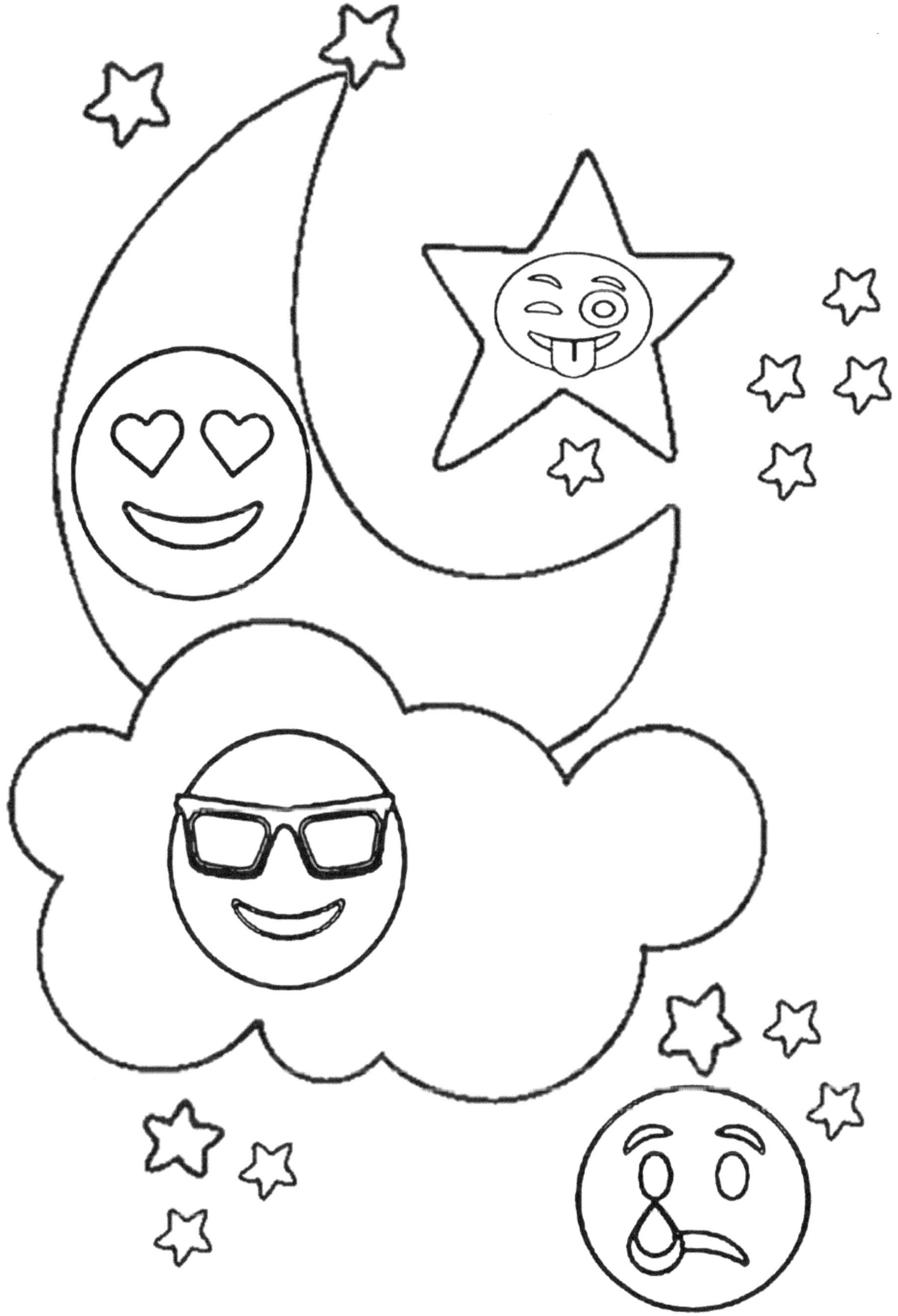

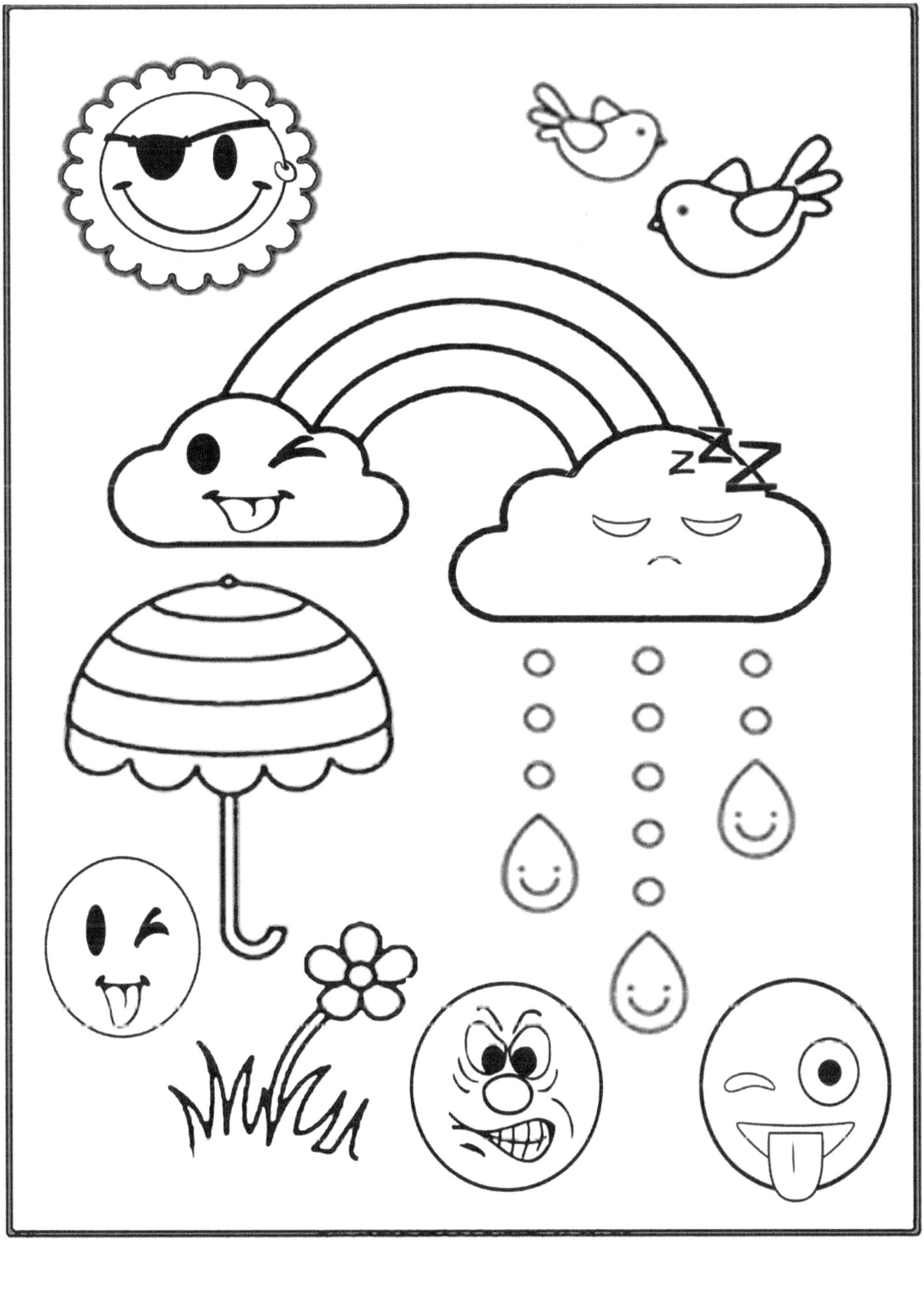
zZZ

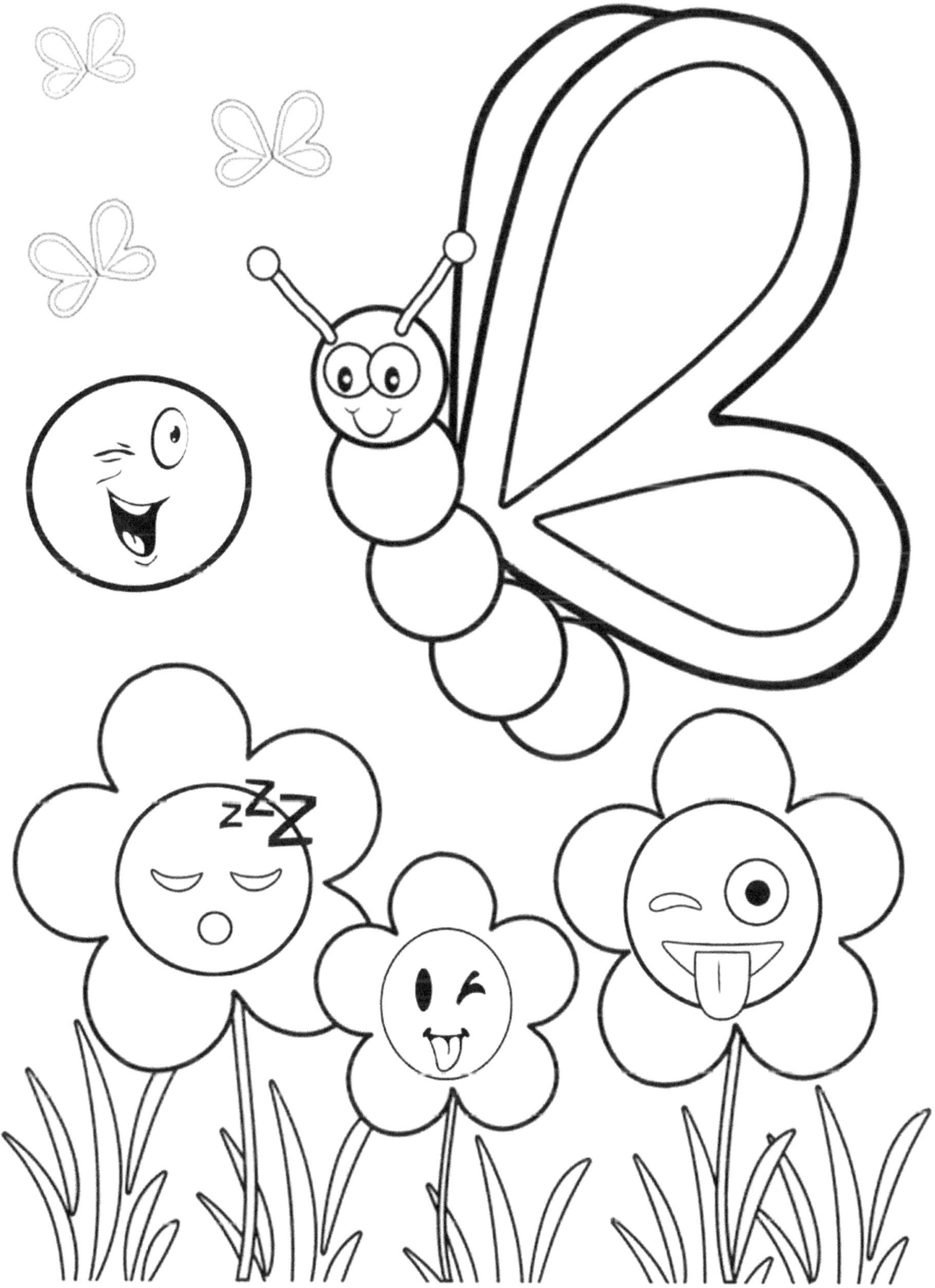
zZZ

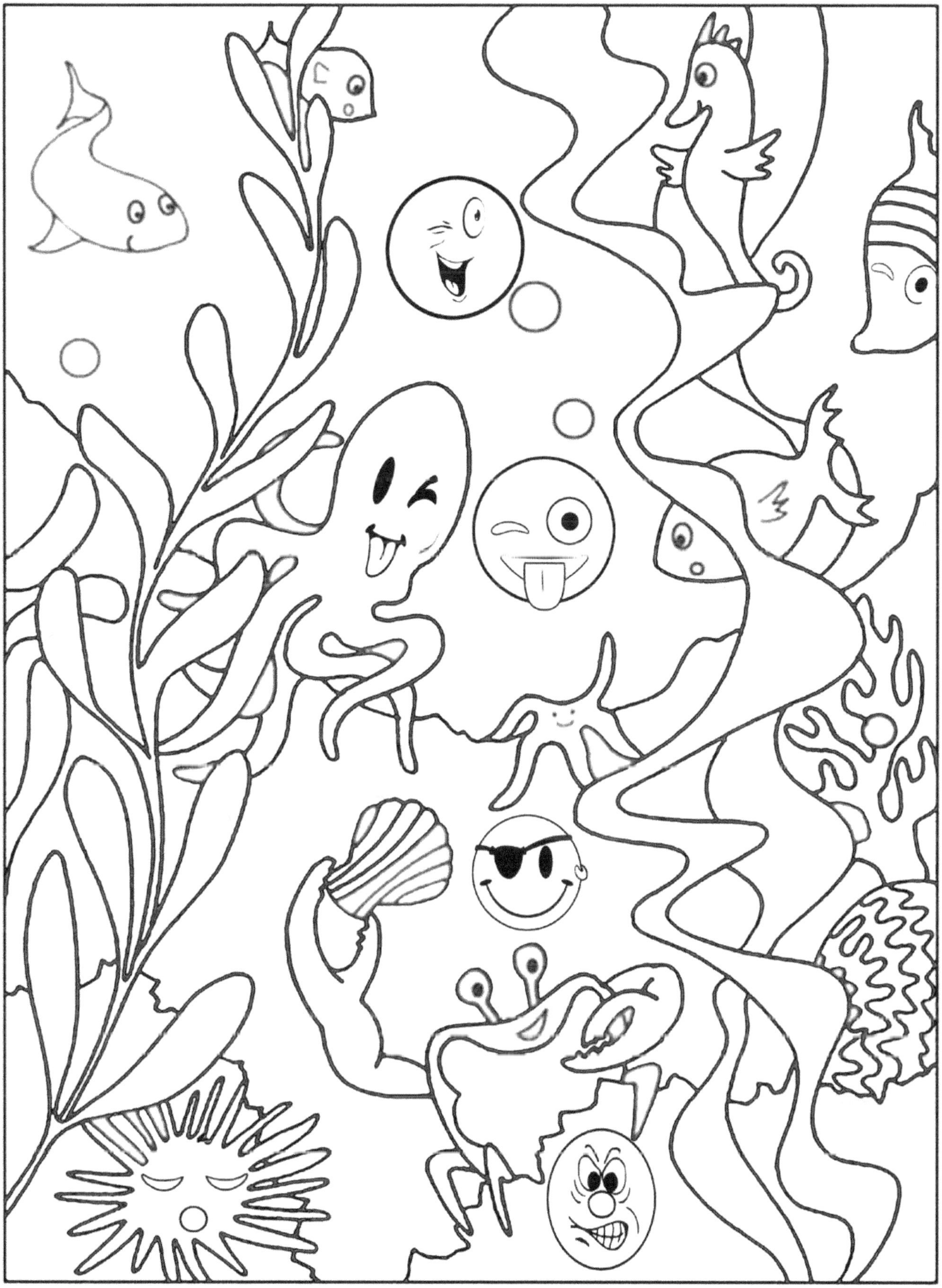

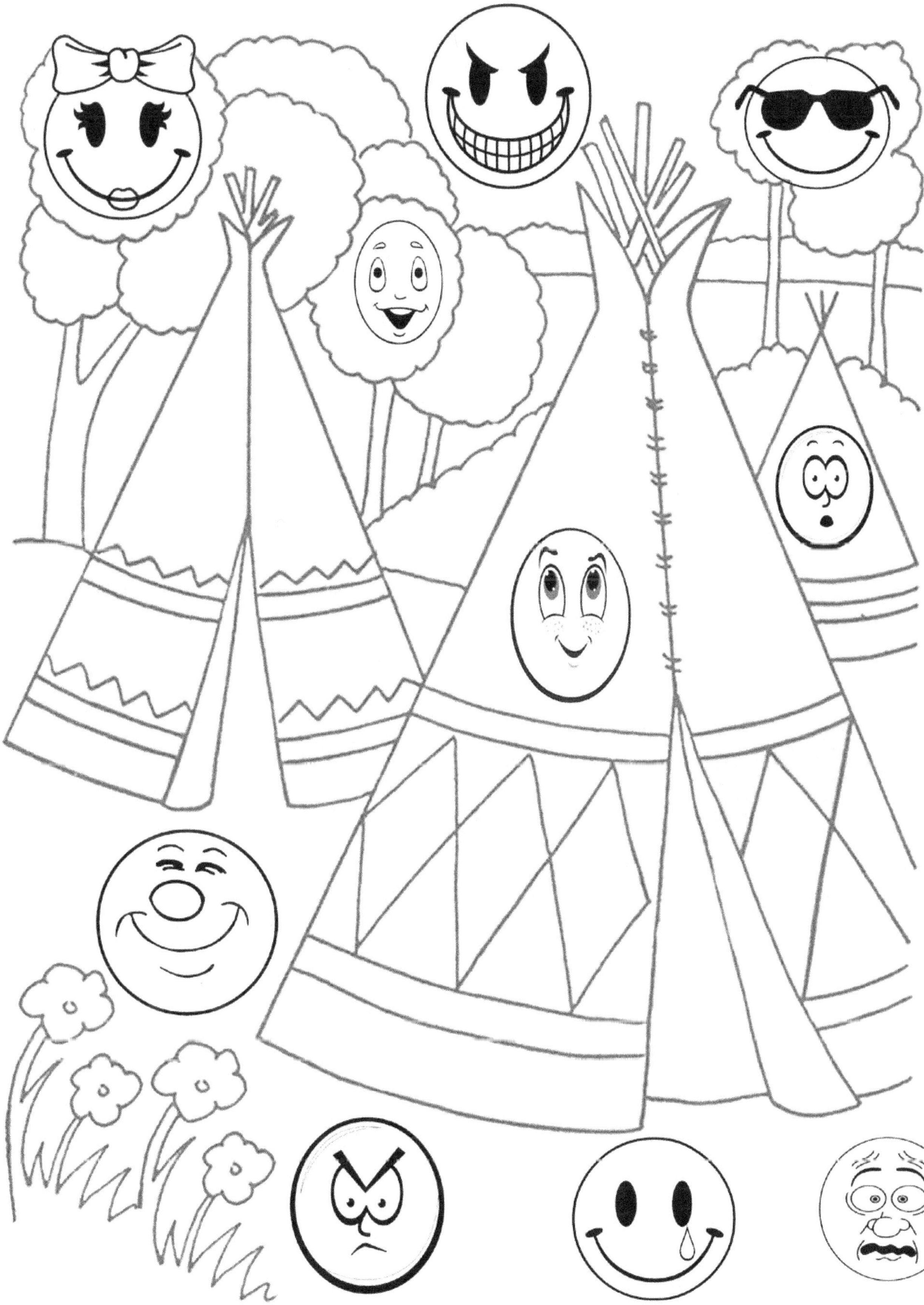

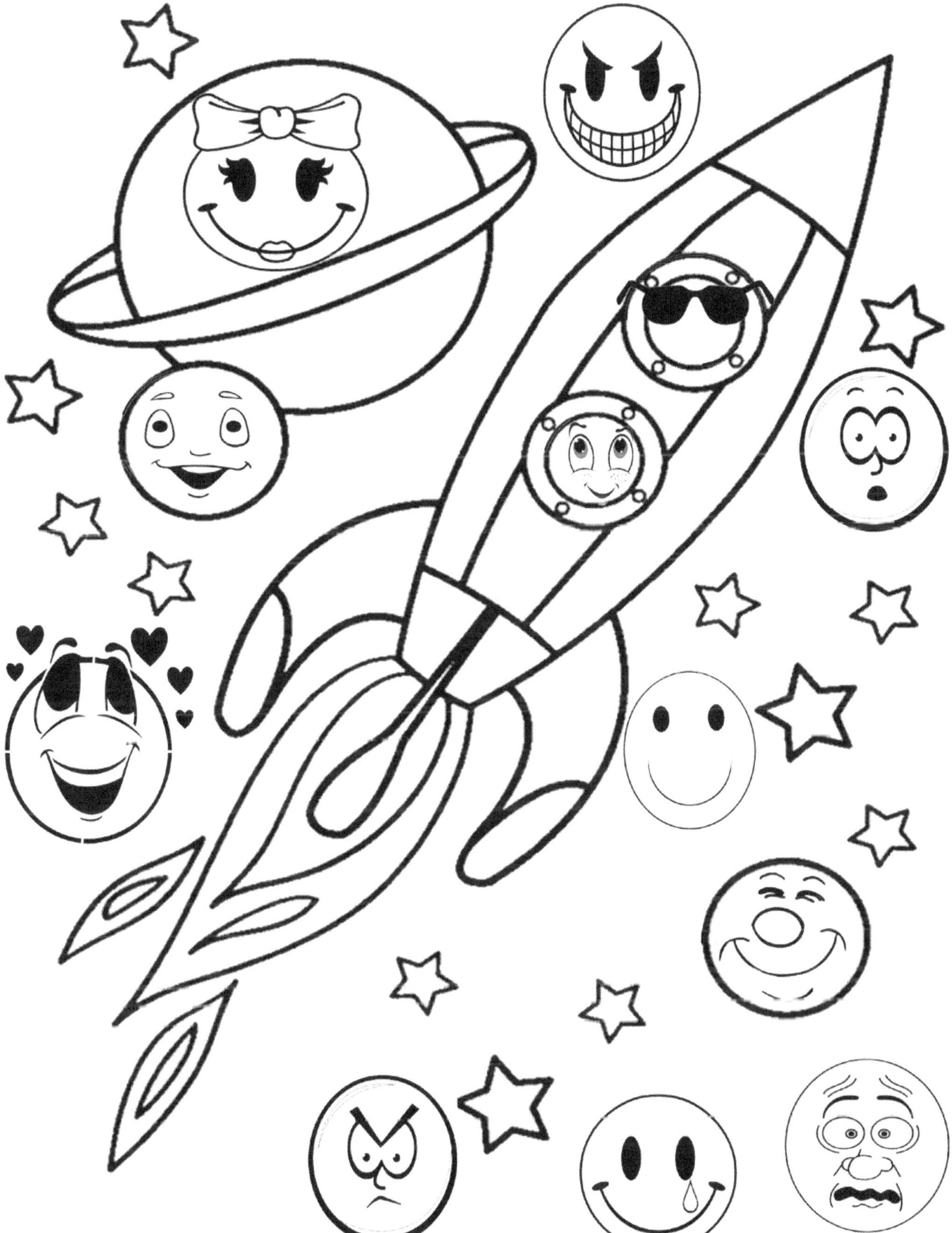

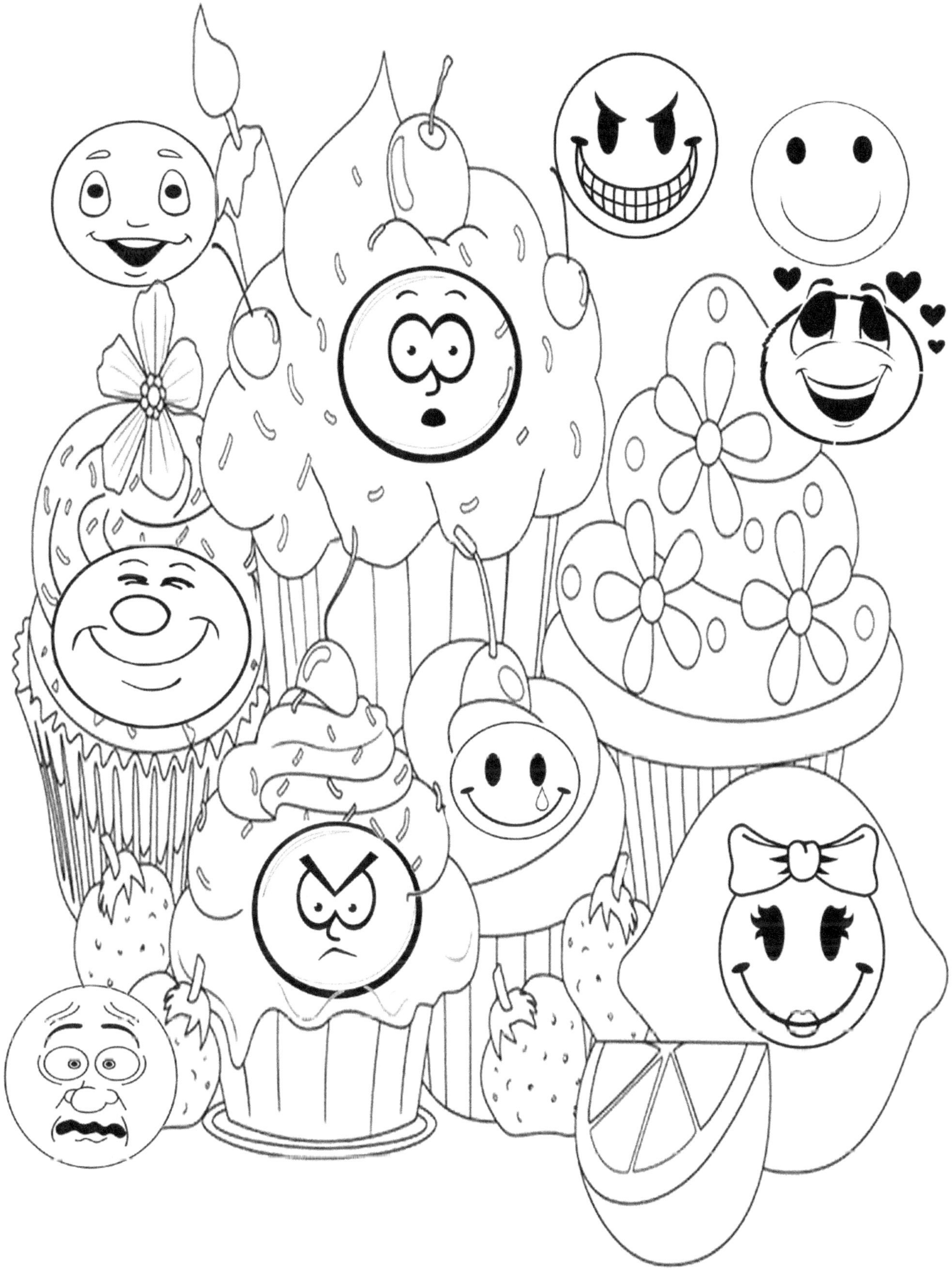

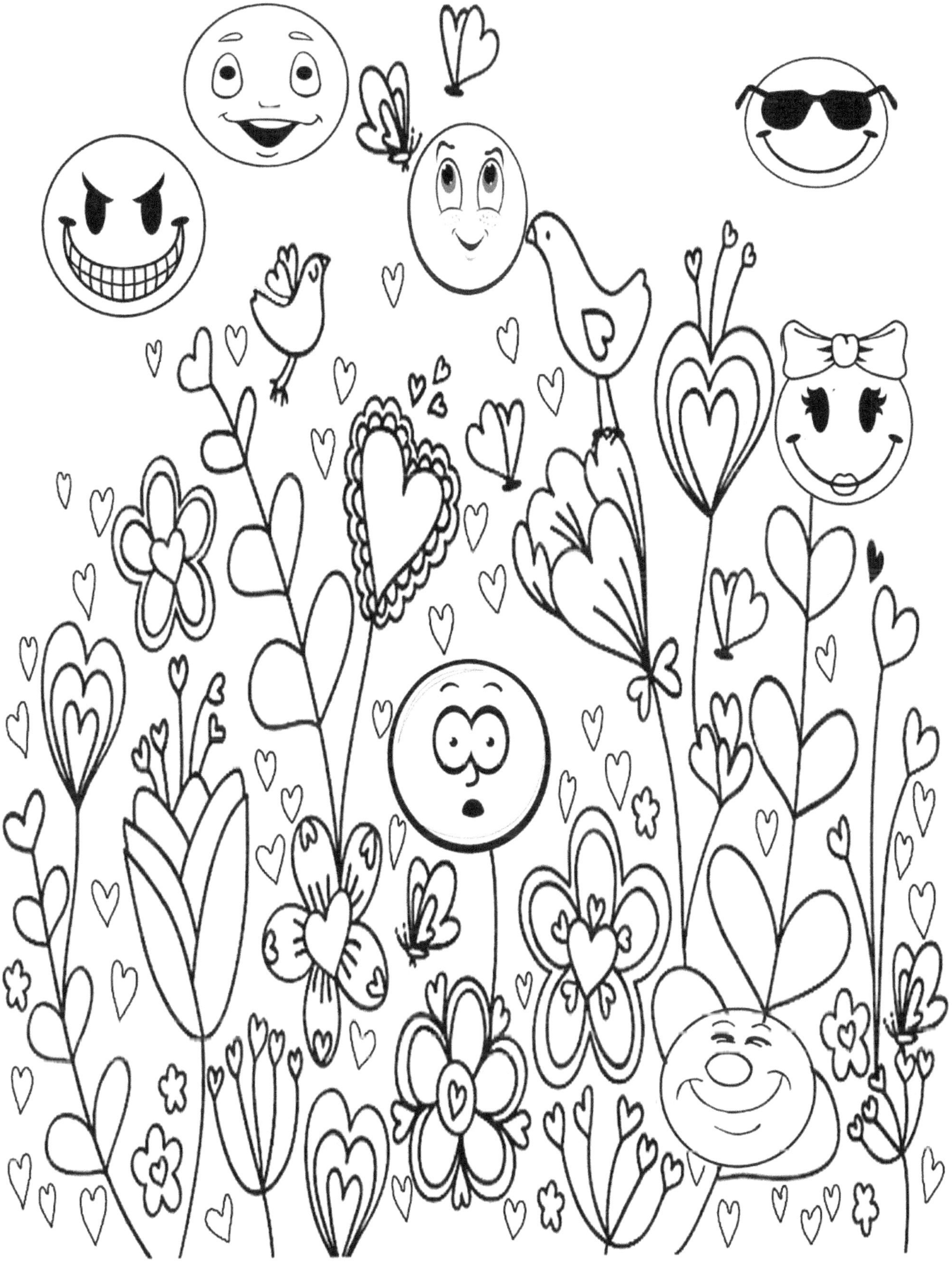

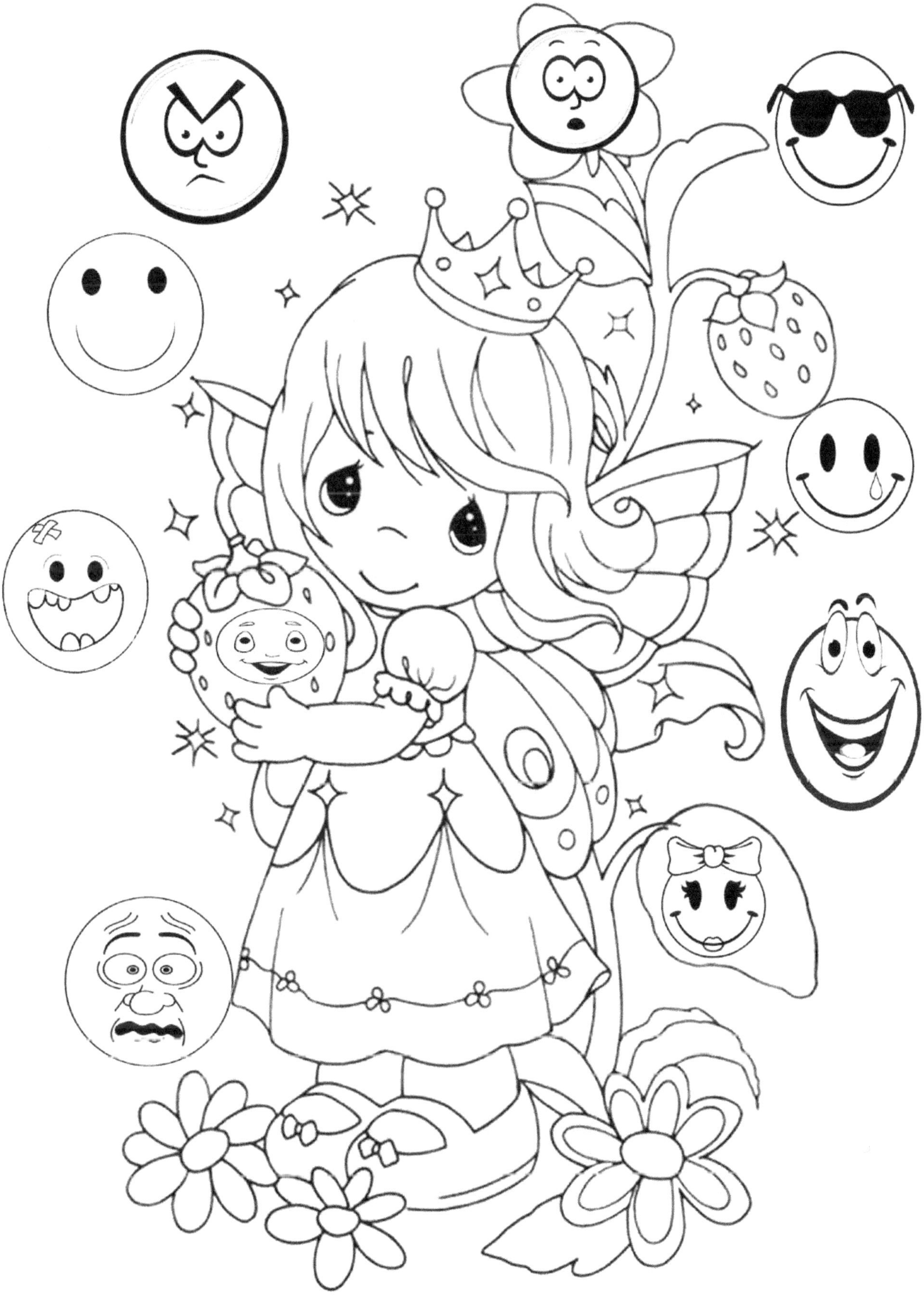

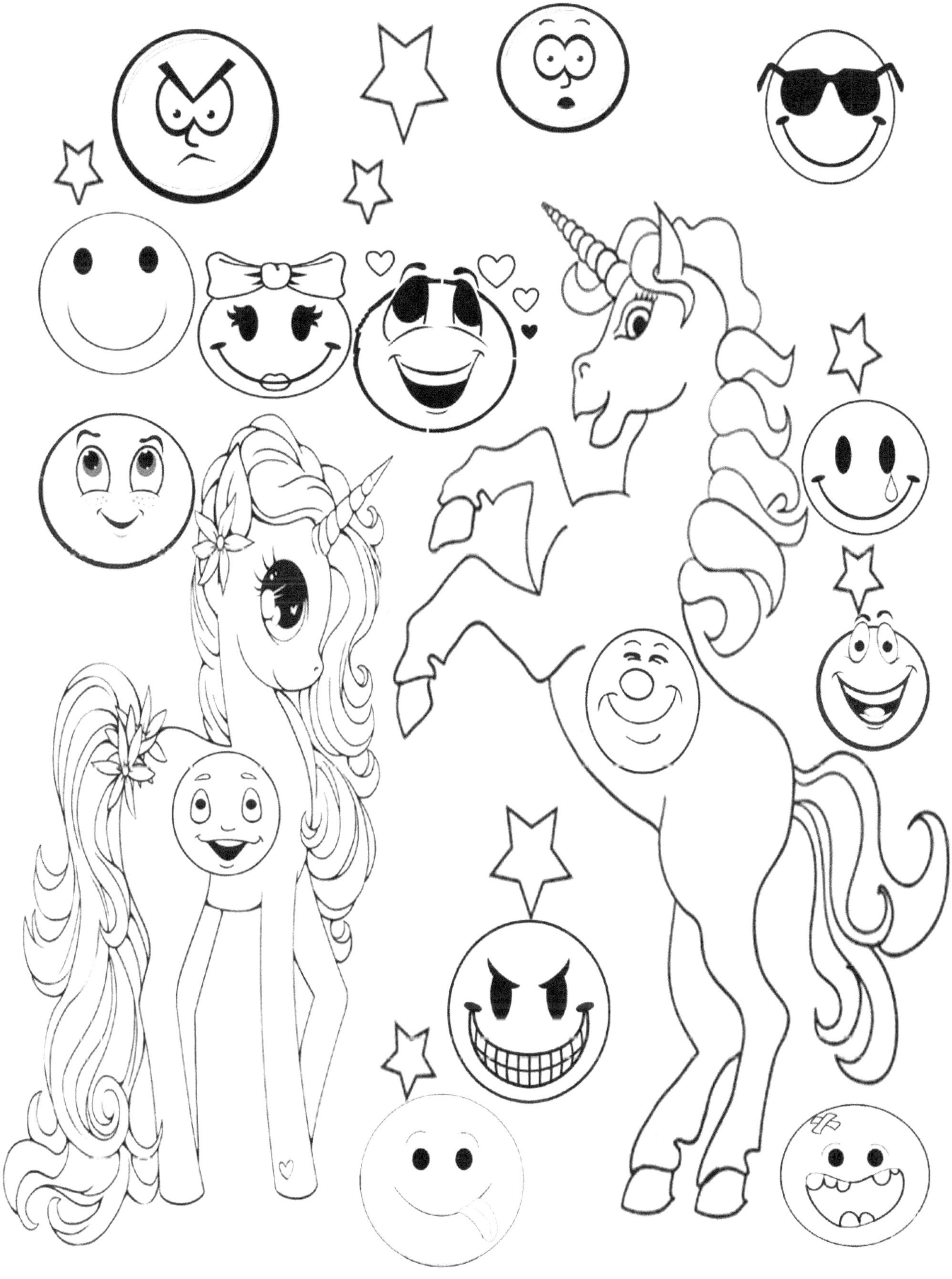

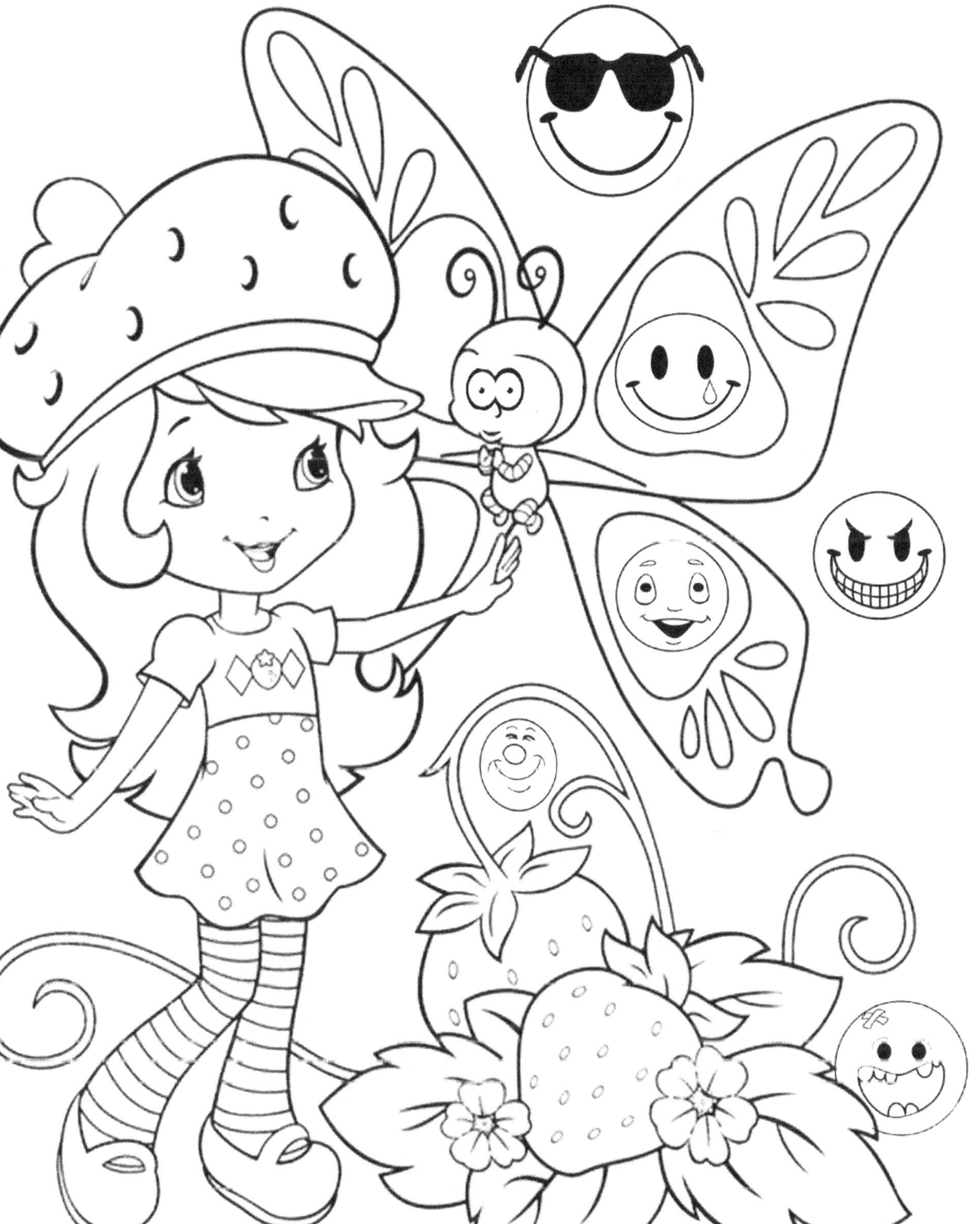

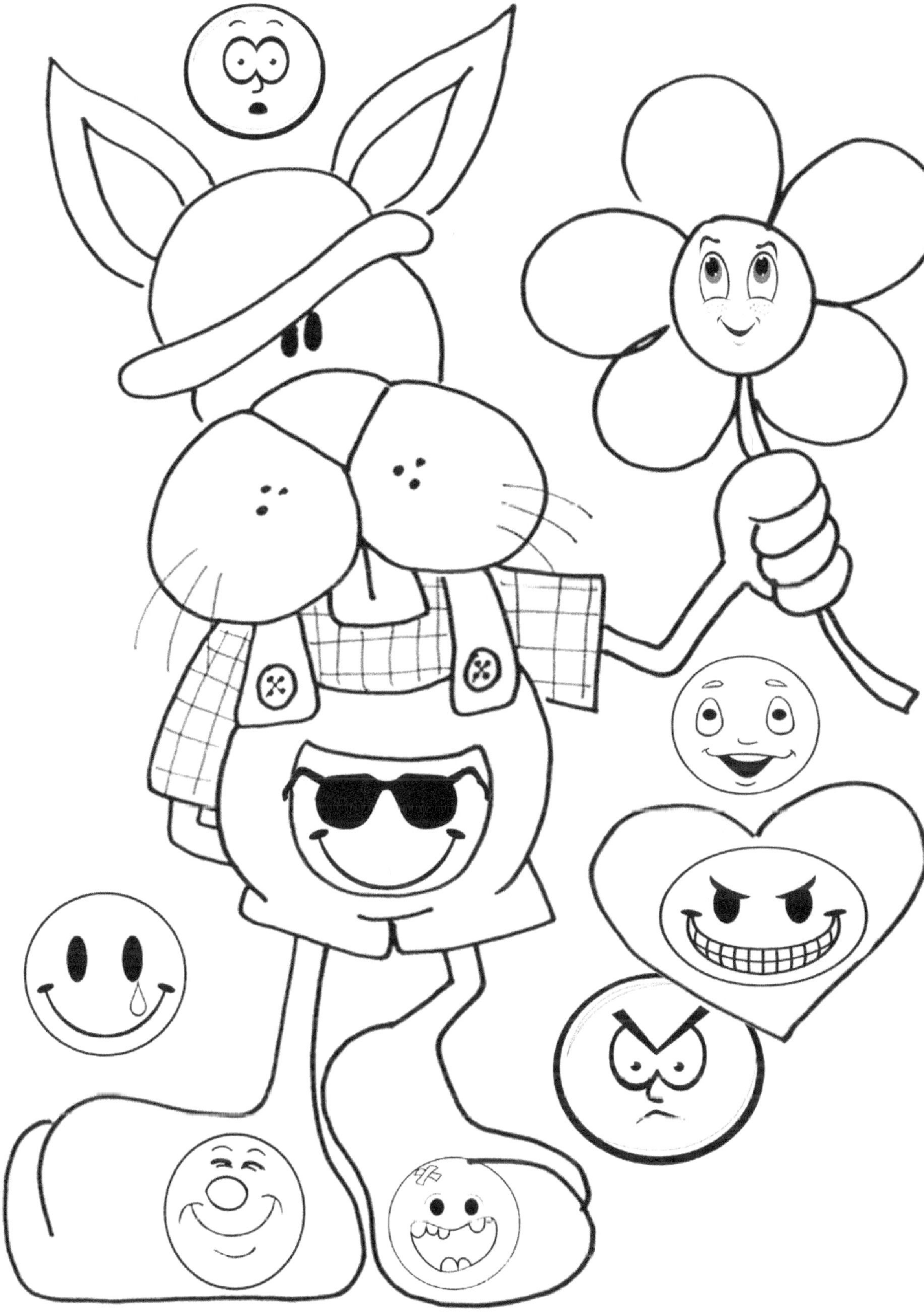

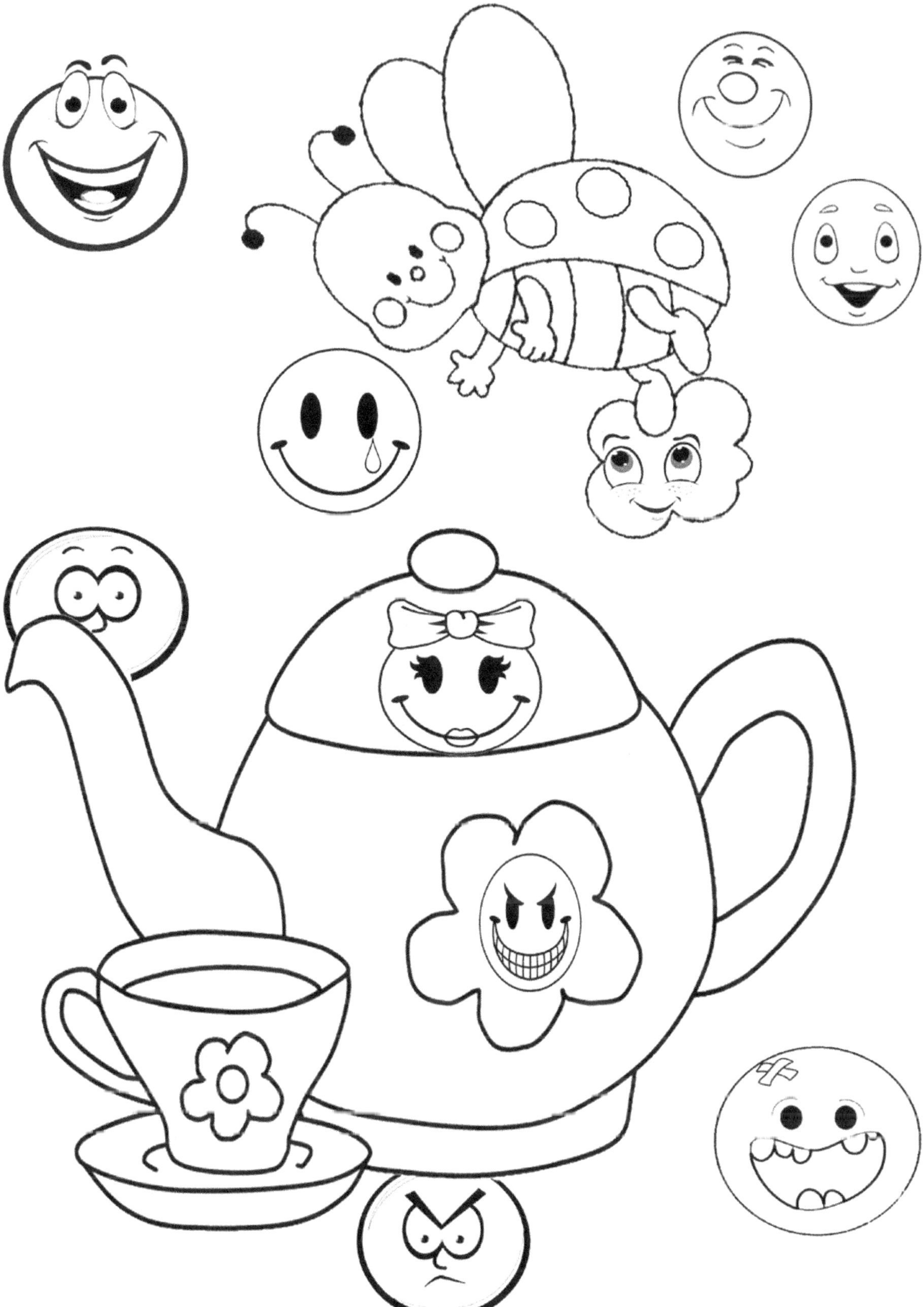

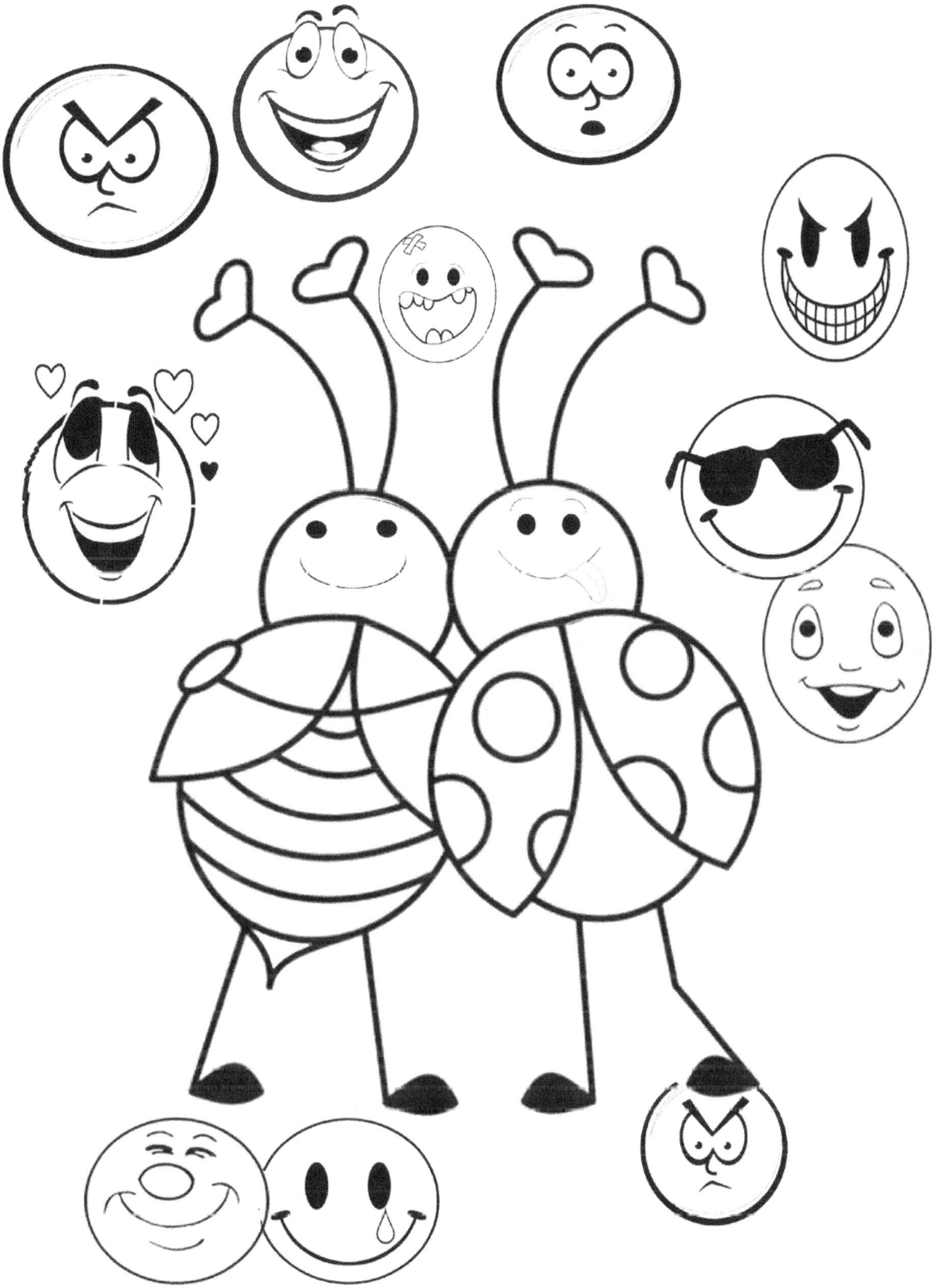

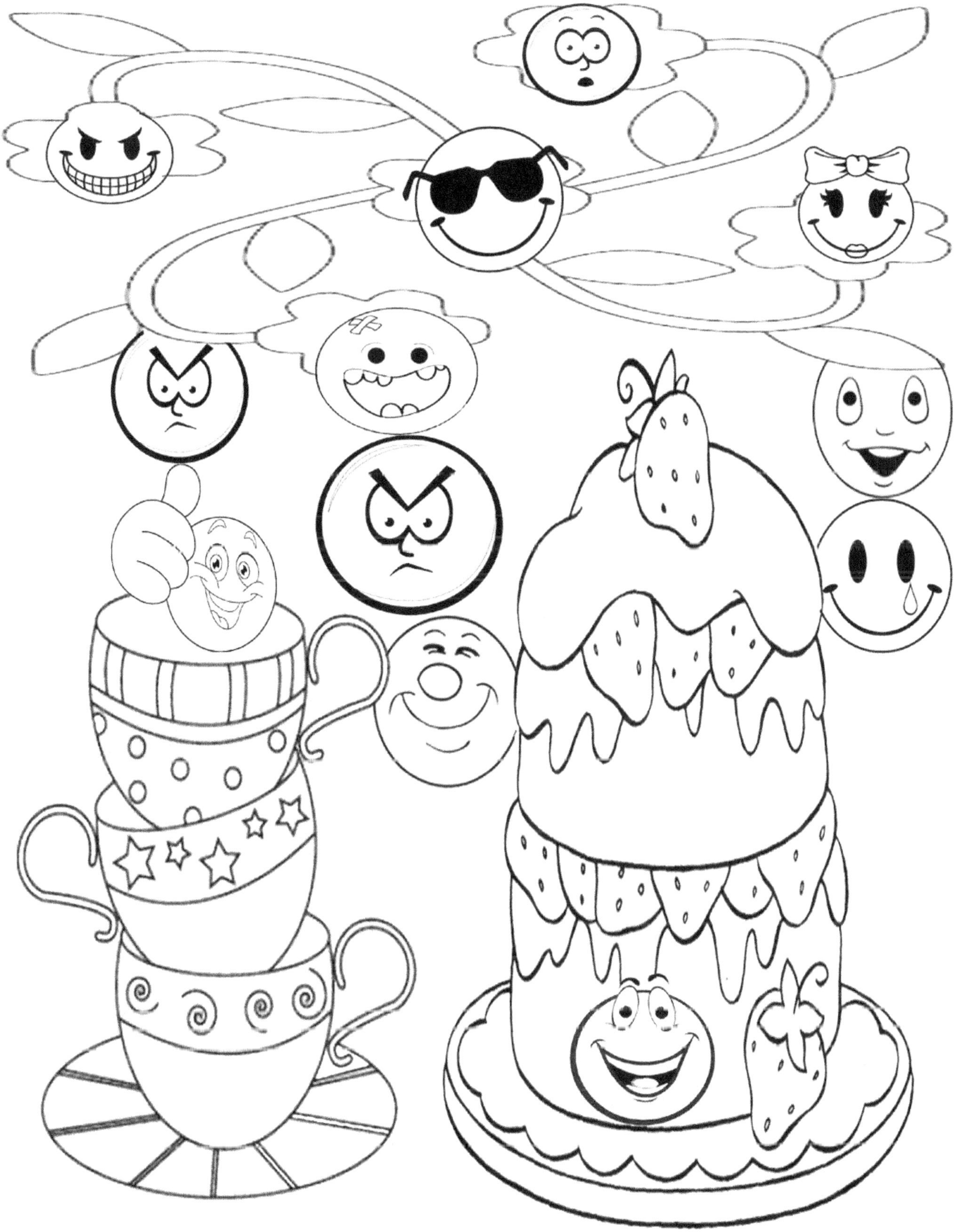

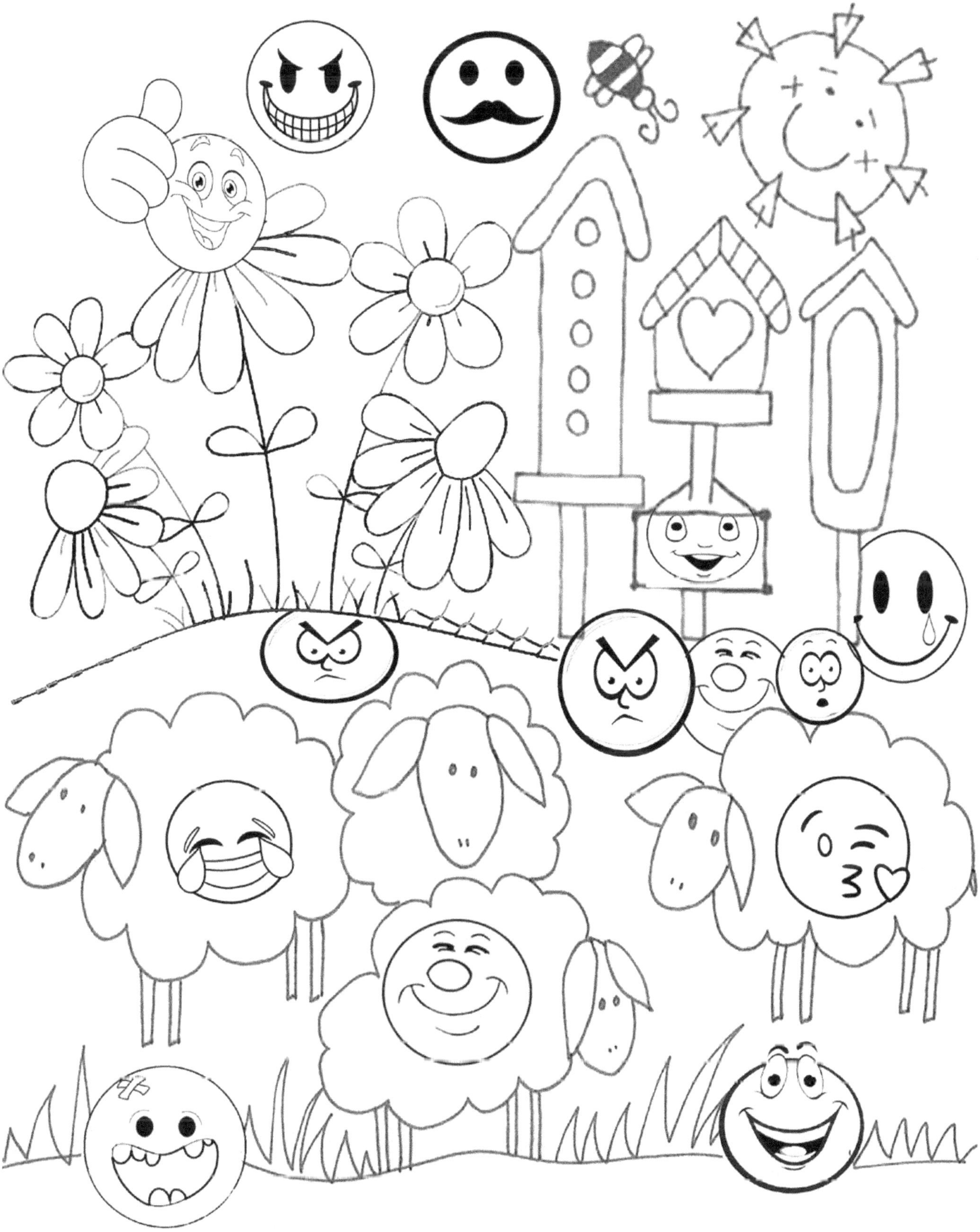

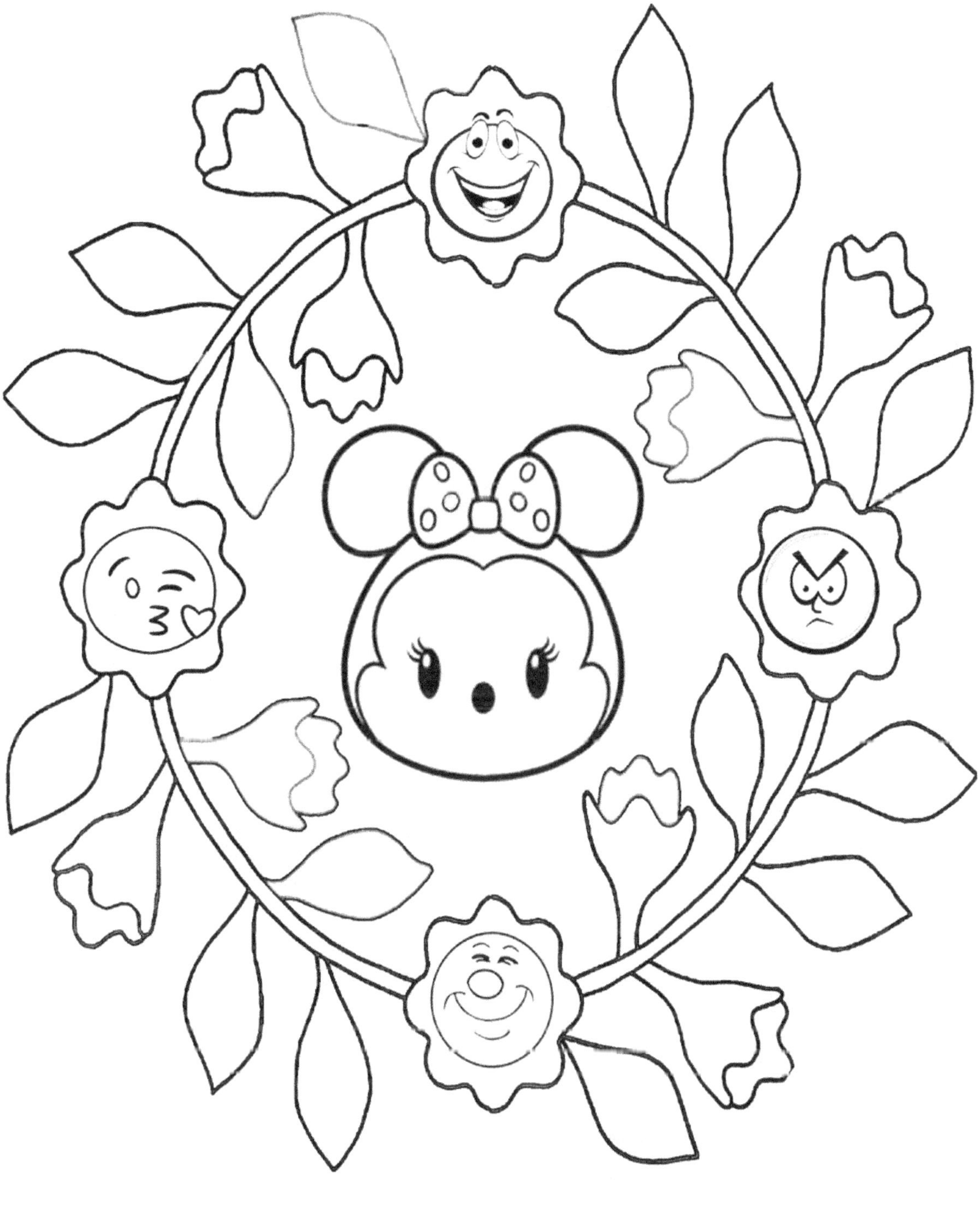

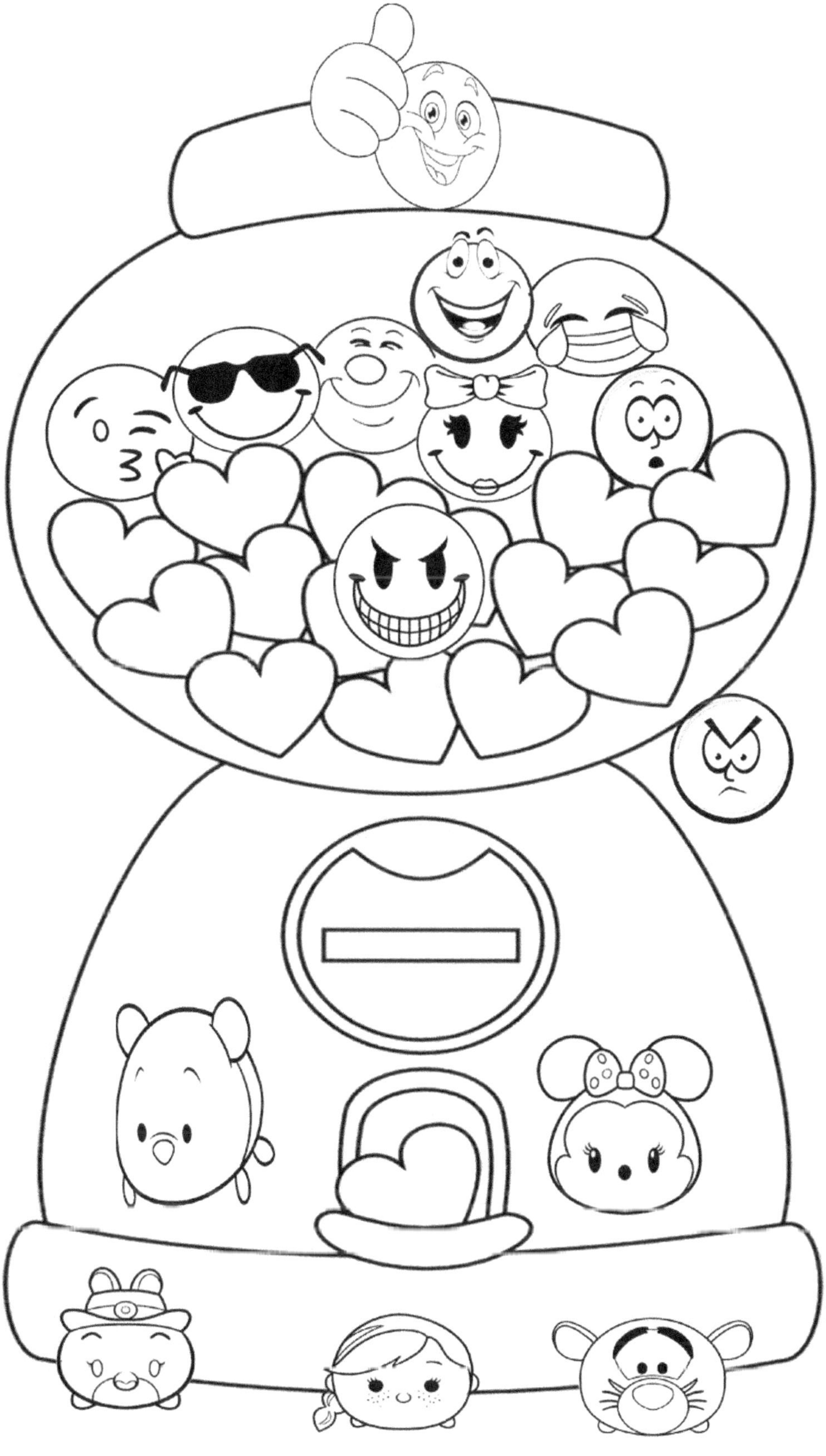

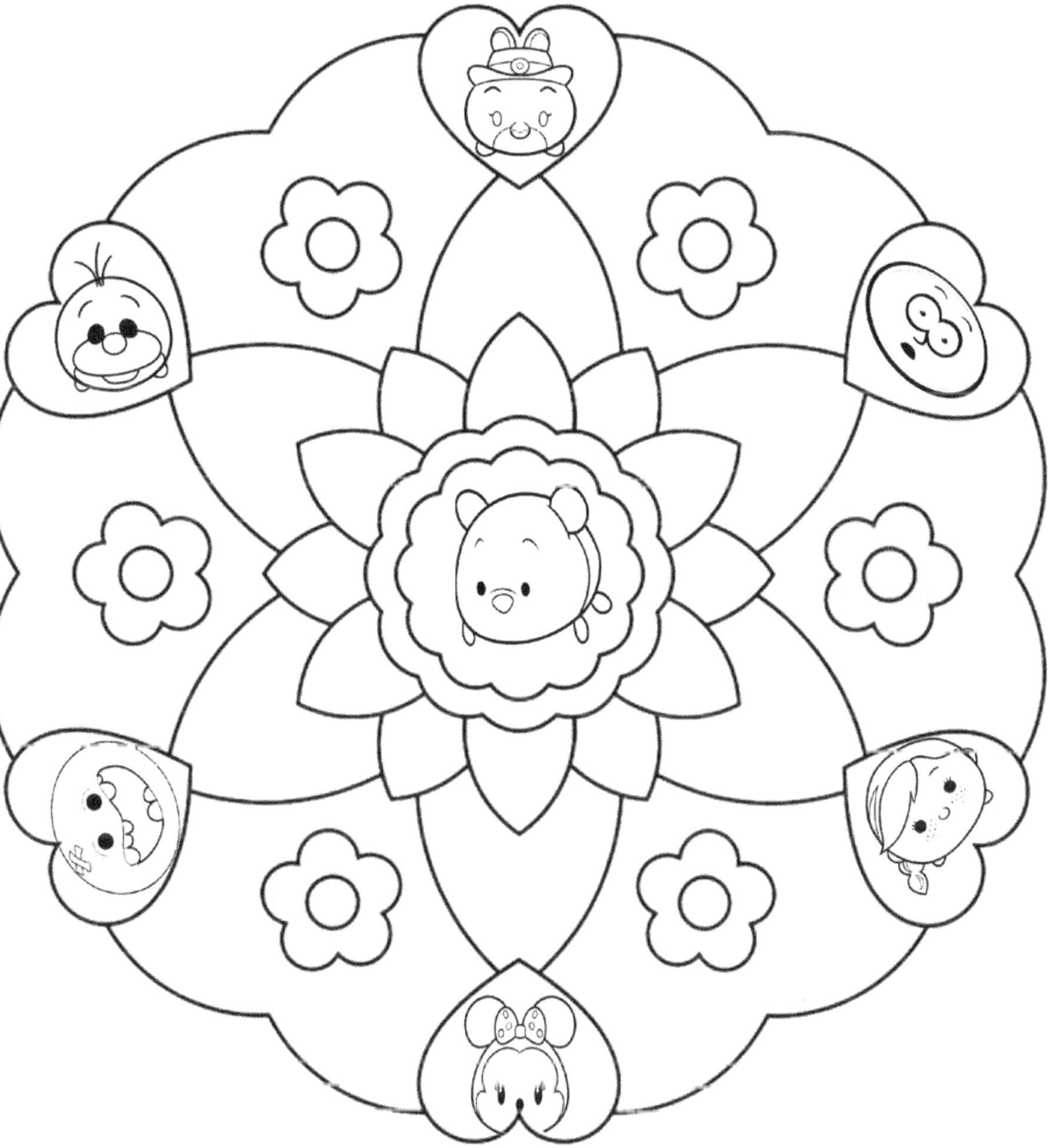

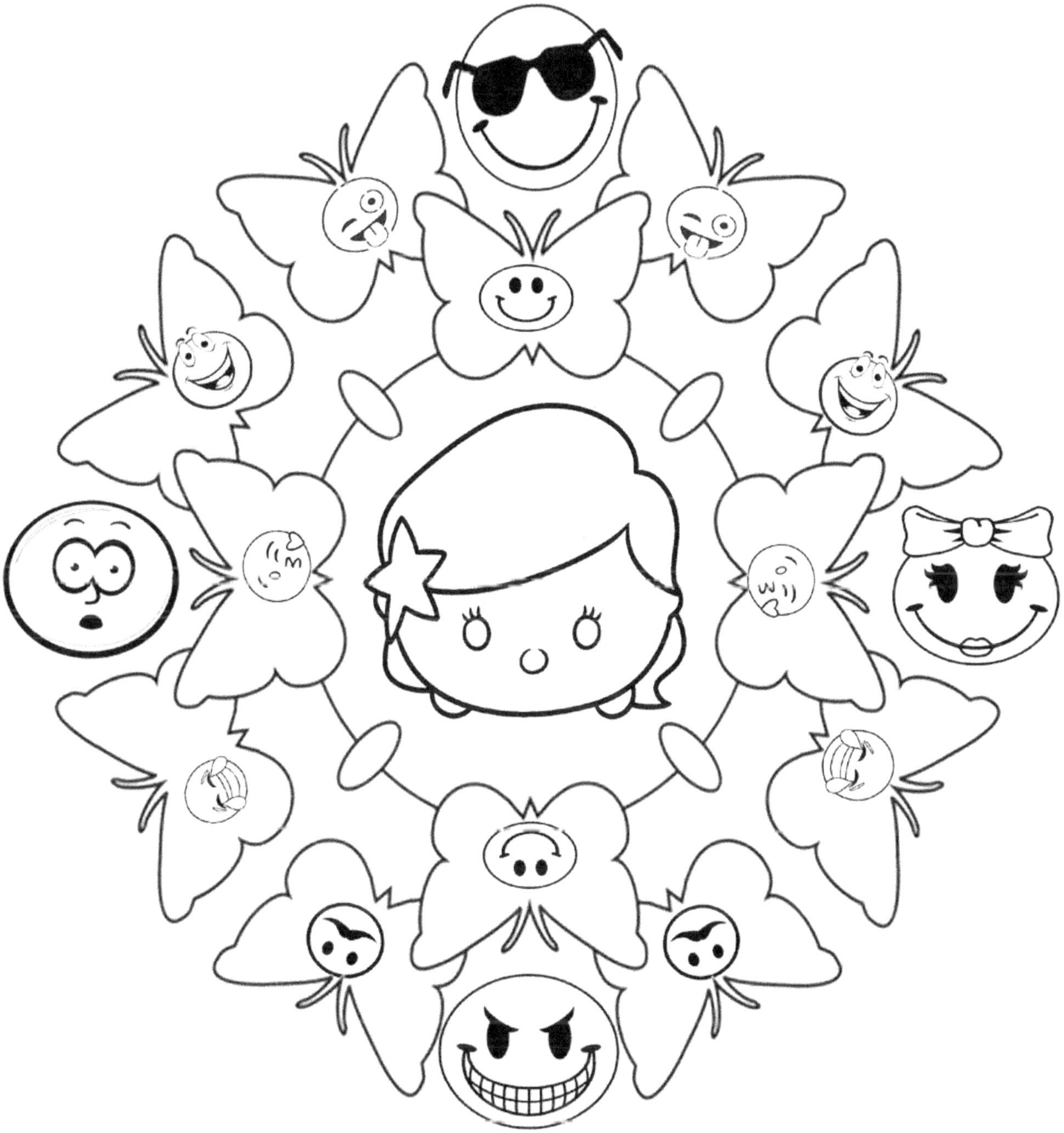

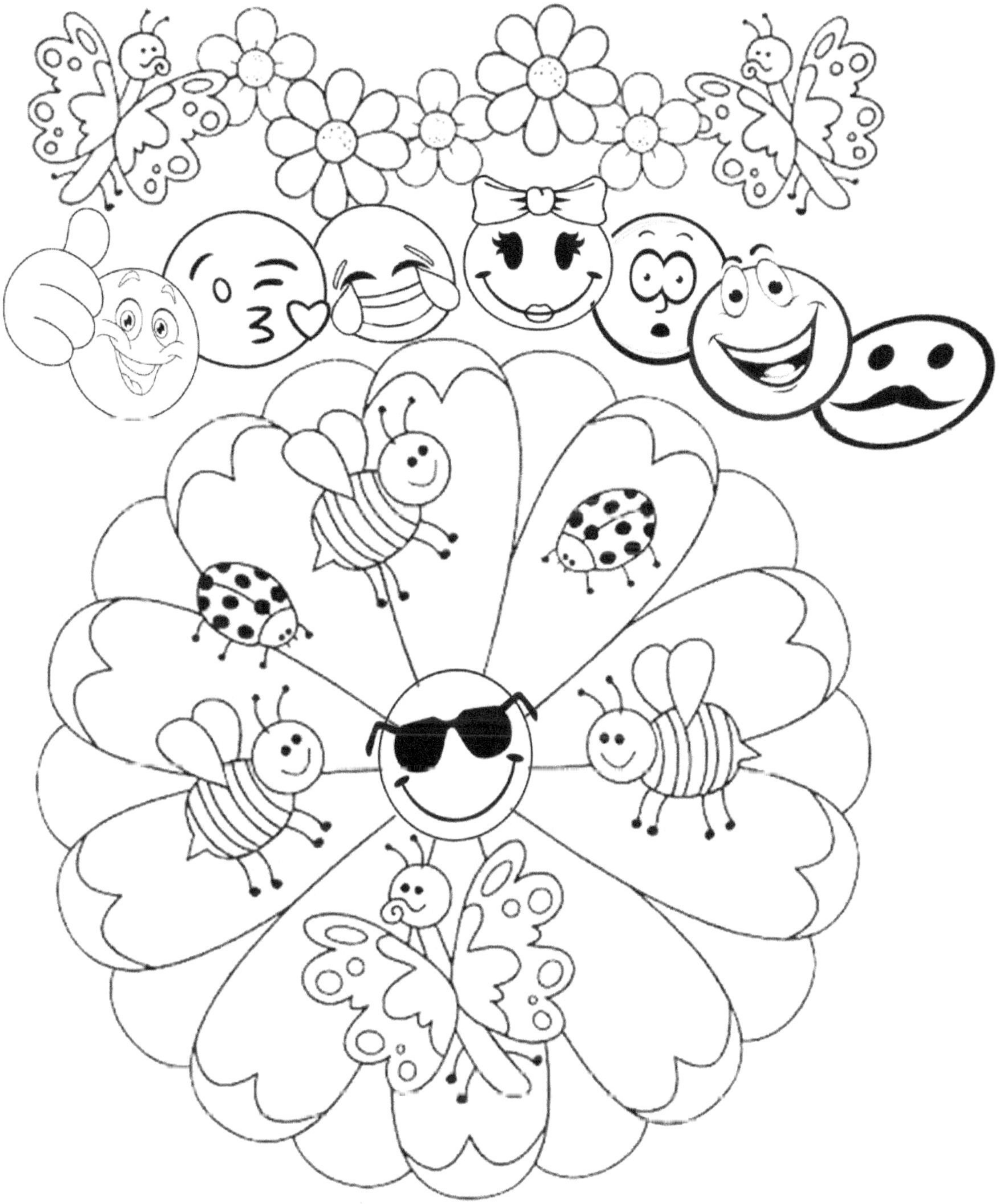

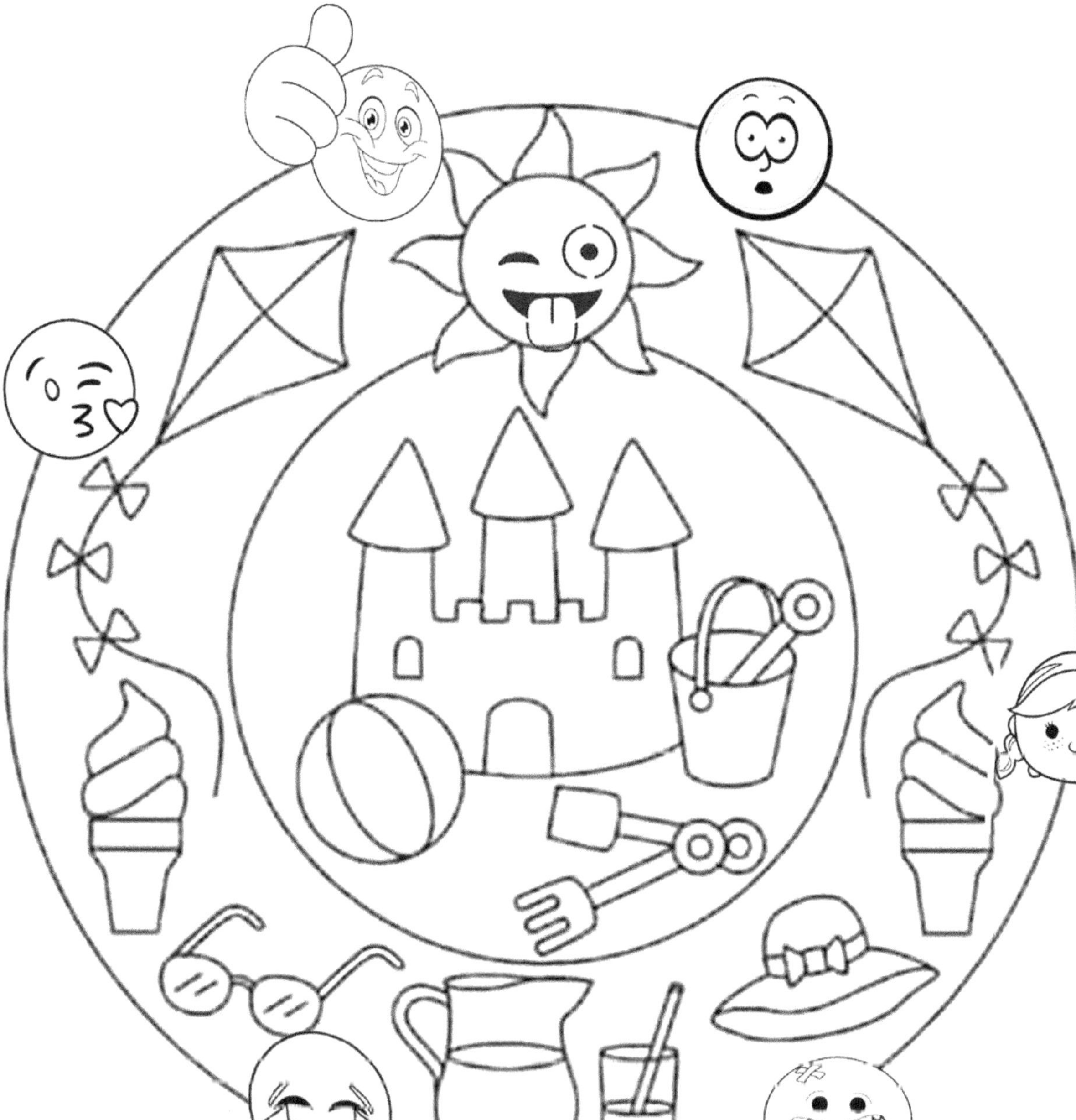

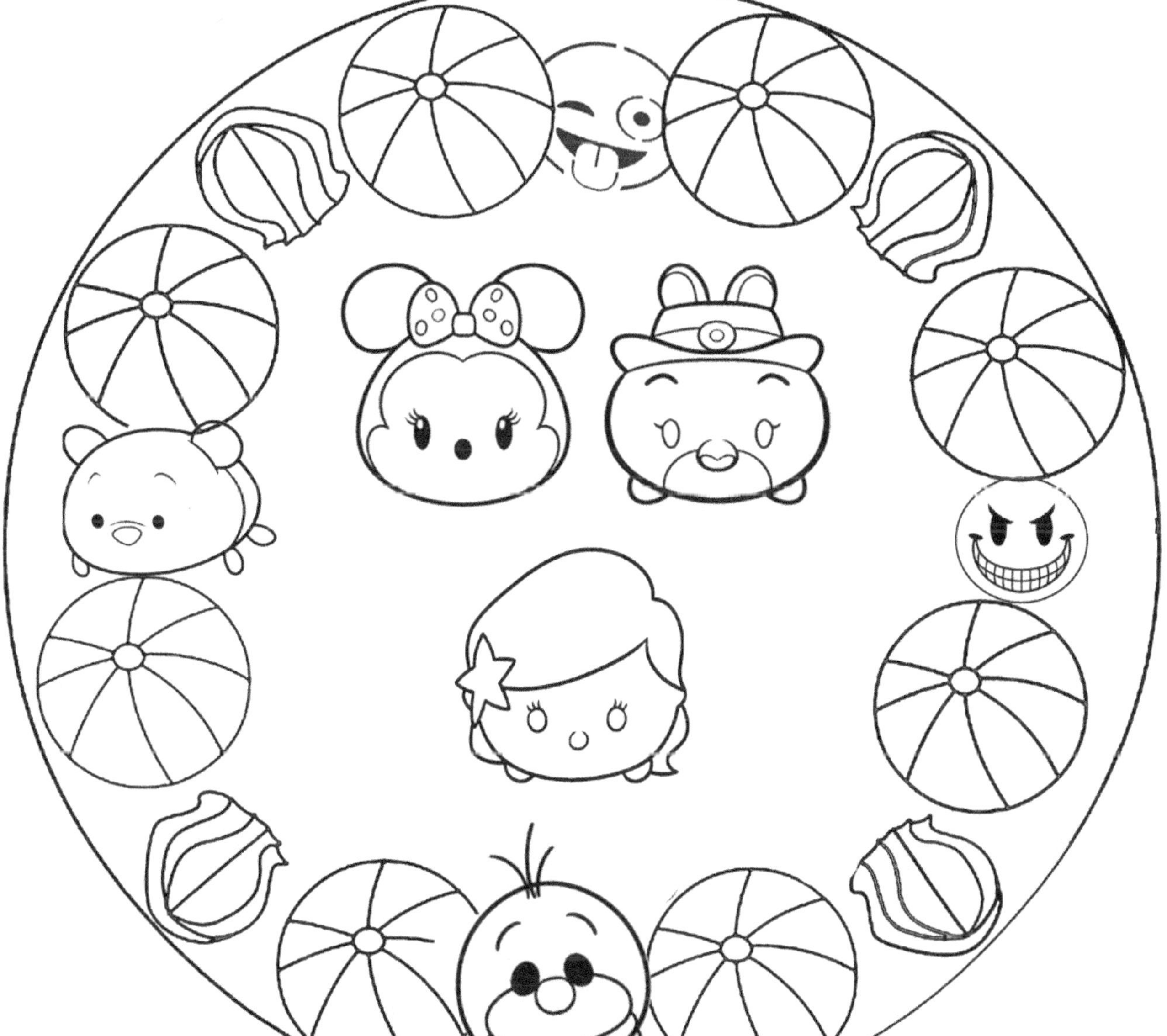

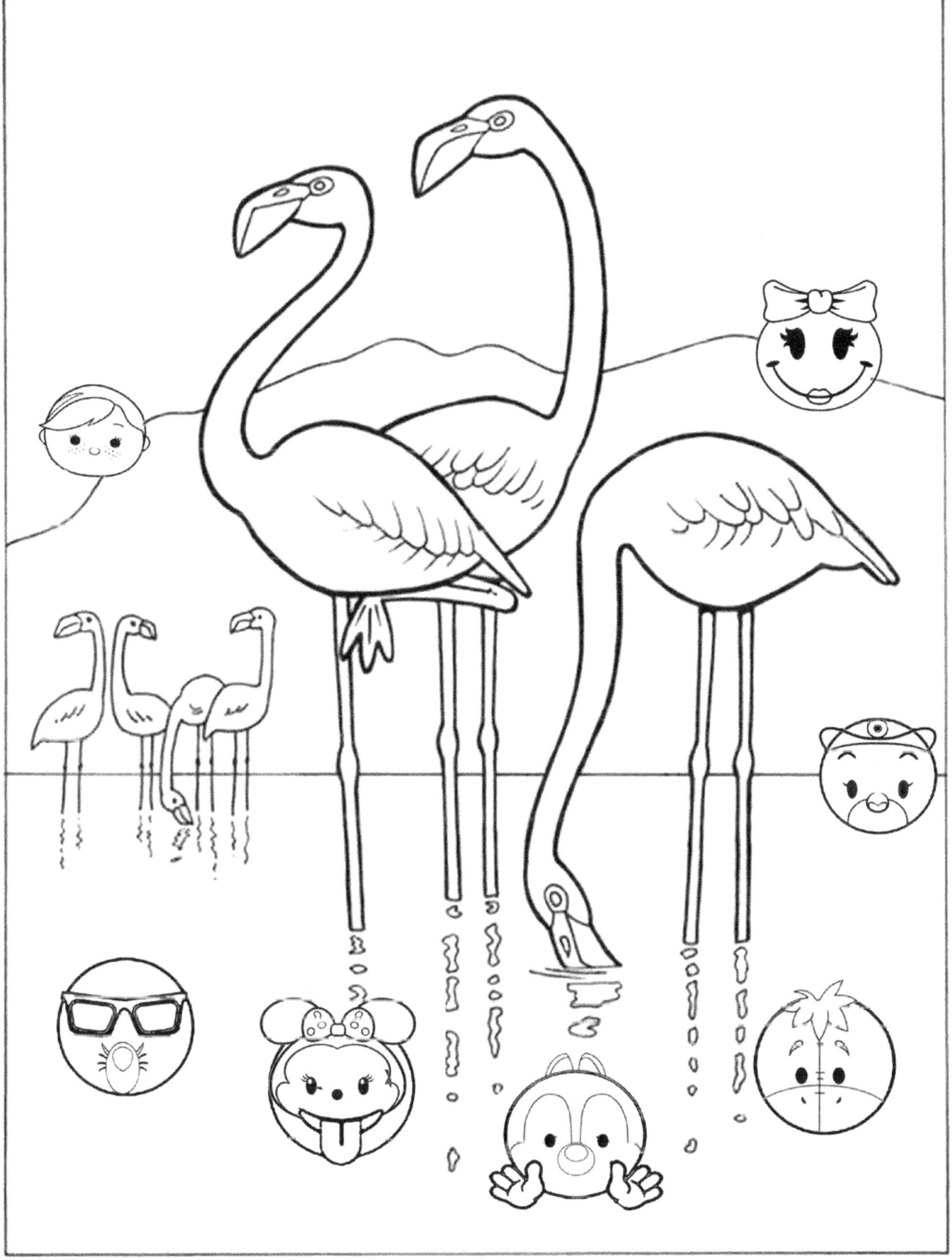

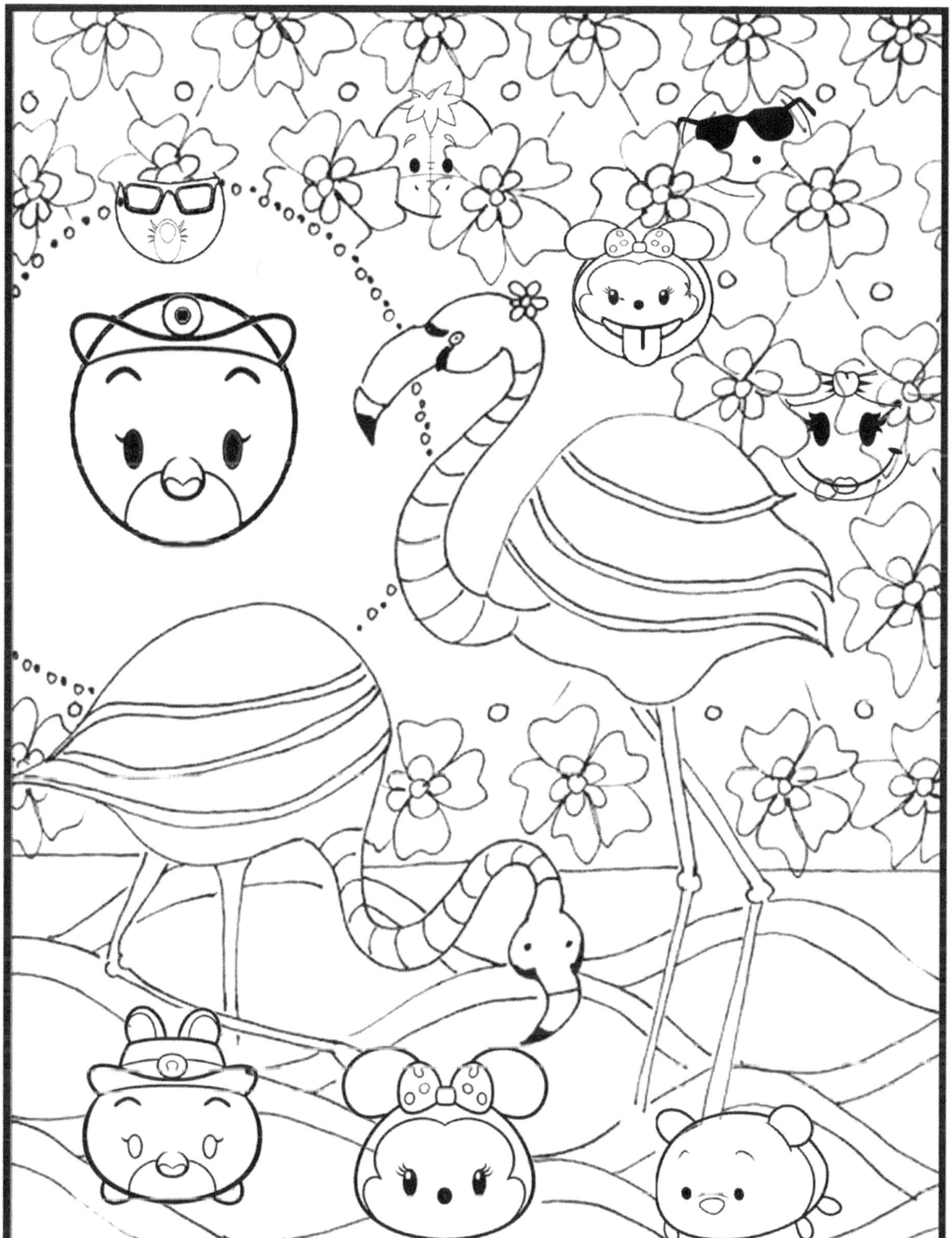

EMOJIS

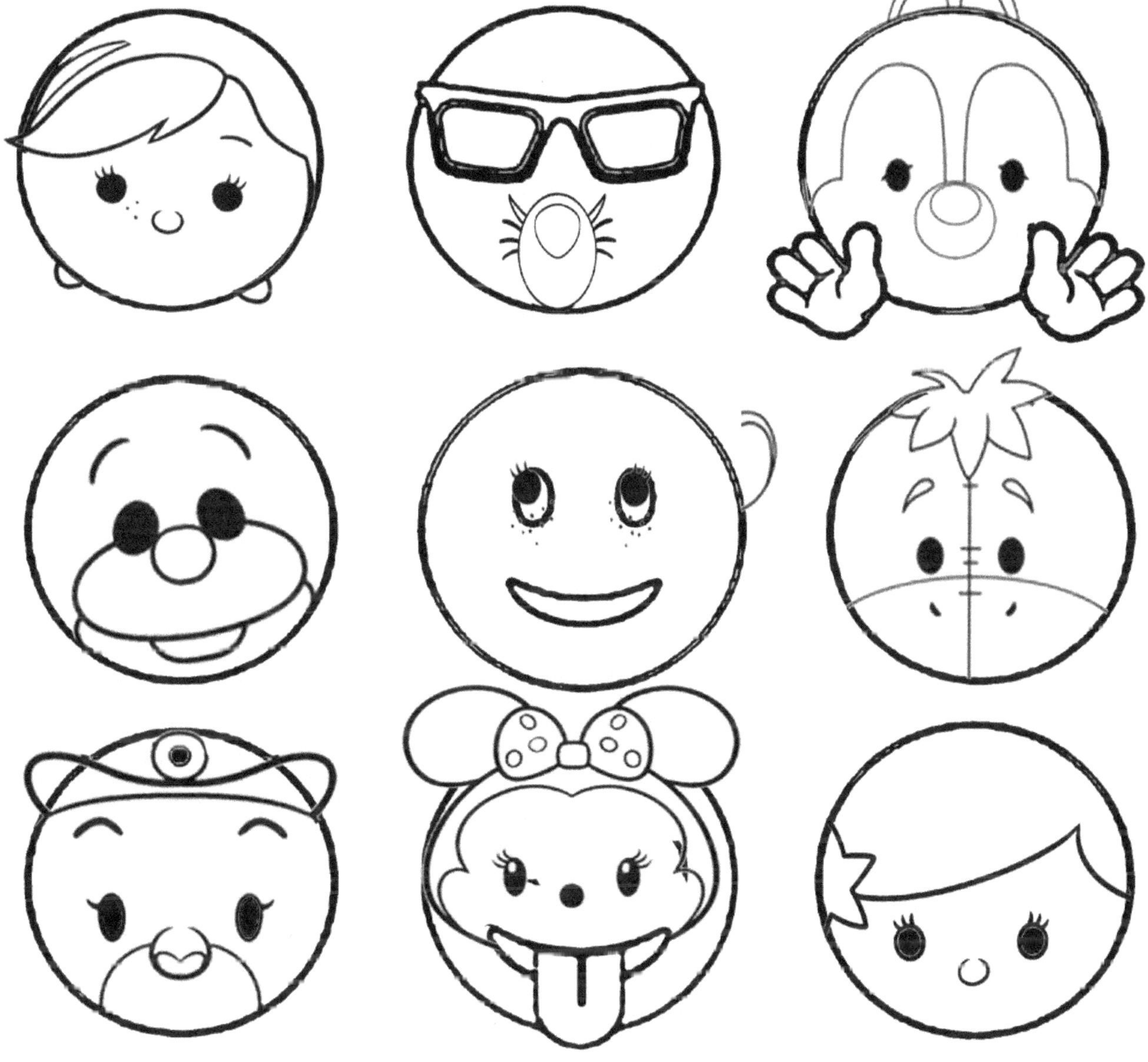

EMOJIS

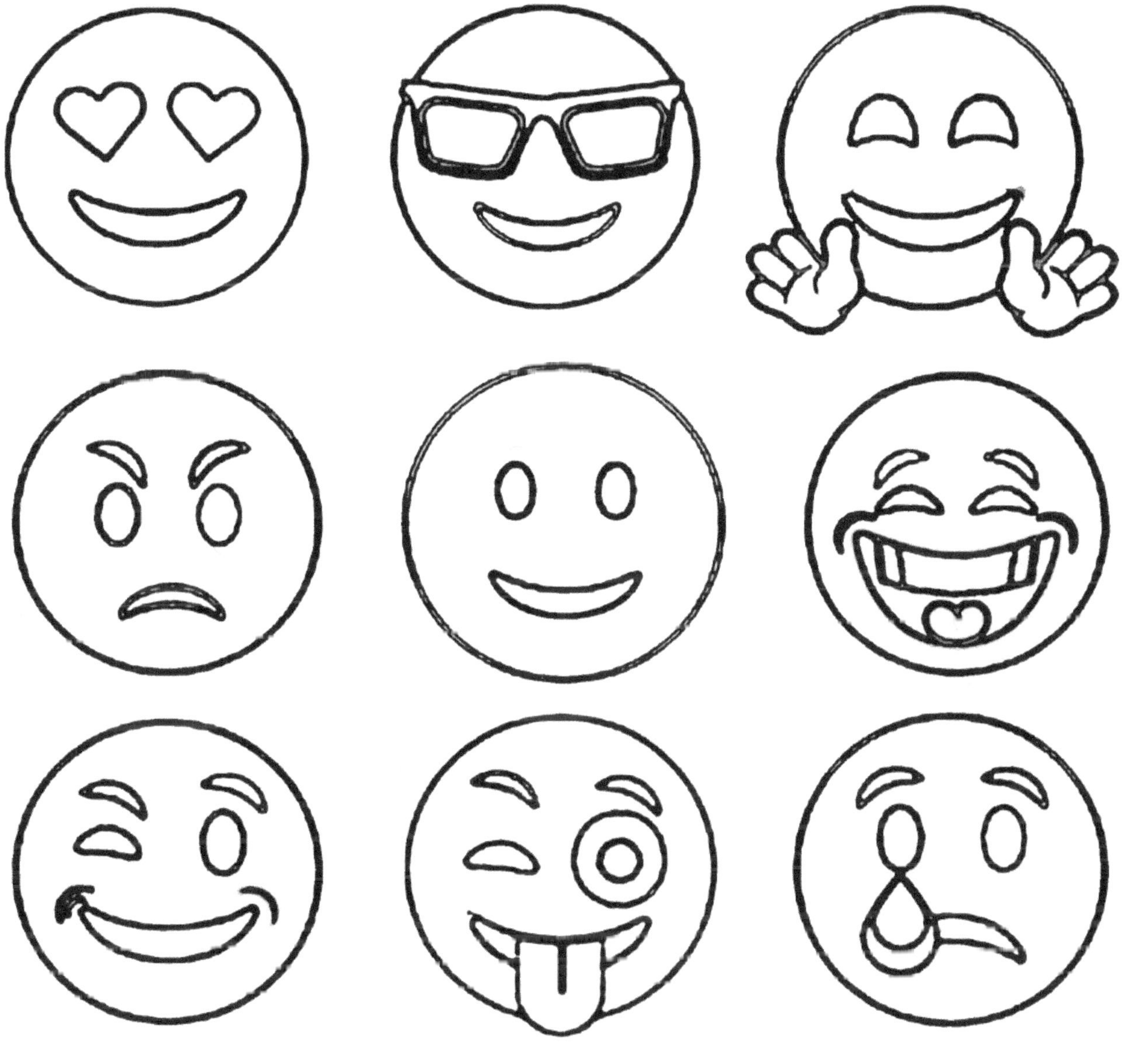

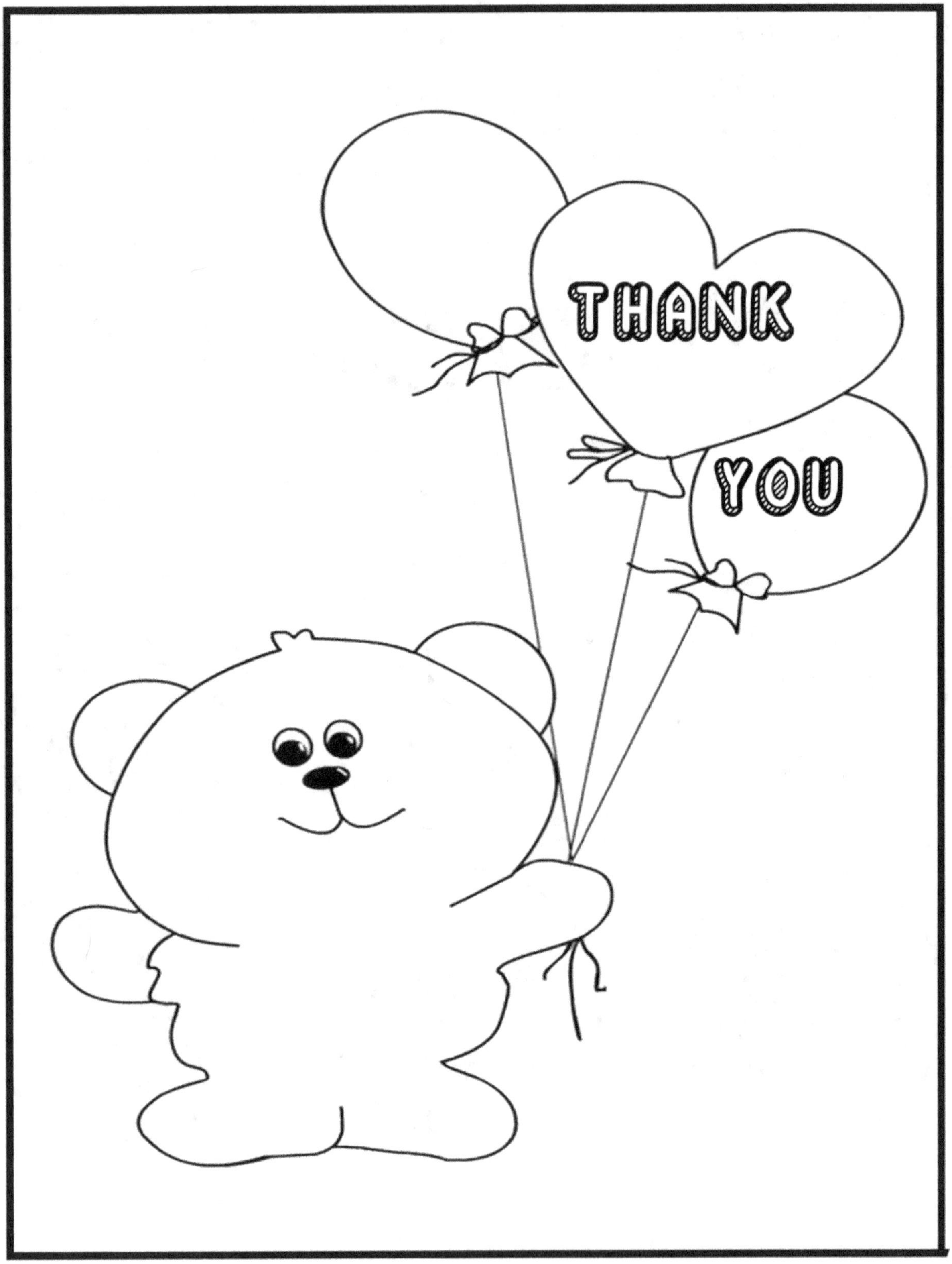
THANK
YOU

www.ingramcontent.com/pod-product-compliance
Lightning Source LLC
Chambersburg PA
CBHW082009230526
45468CB00023B/2905
* 9 7 8 1 9 8 3 5 5 4 6 8 1 *